The Mask of State: Watergate Portraits

Books by Mary McCarthy

The Company She Keeps

The Oasis

Cast a Cold Eye

The Groves of Academe

A Charmed Life

Memories of a Catholic Girlhood

Venice Observed

The Stones of Florence

On the Contrary

The Group

Mary McCarthy's Theatre Chronicles

The Writing on the Wall

Birds of America

The Seventeenth Degree

The Mask of State: Watergate Portraits

Mary McCarthy

The Mask of State: Watergate Portraits

A Harvest Book

Harcourt Brace Jovanovich
New York and London

To the Honorable Sam J. Ervin, Jr.

". . . with russet yeas and honest kersey noes."

Library of Congress Cataloging in Publication Data

McCarthy, Mary Therese, date
The mask of state.

(A Harvest book, HB 283)
1. Watergate Affair, 1972-   I. Title.
E860.M32   1975   364.1'32'0973   74-26953
ISBN 0-15-657302-4

First Harvest edition 1975

A B C D E F G H I J

Contents

Six of the nine chapters in this book were written as reports from Washington for *The Observer*, London, and the dates given are those of their original publication. The texts, which were originally sent by cable, have been greatly revised and amplified. The chapters "Notes of a Watergate Resident" and "Always That Doubt" and a postscript on the pardon were written for *The New York Review of Books*.

The Athlete
of
Evasion
and the
Prodigal
Son

June 17, 1973

This April, when the Watergate revelations broke, I was traveling across America. Almost more amazing than the daily disclosures themselves was the evidence that the story was being told, democratically, to the entire population, which was discussing it, democratically, as if at a town meeting. Leaving New York and flying westward, to Minneapolis, Seattle, then down to Carmel Valley, California, I had expected to lose whole chapters of the story, since this country, on the whole, outside of a few sophisticated cities —New York, Washington, Los Angeles, St. Louis—is poorly informed by its press. Wire service dispatches, usually cut and mangled, a mixed bag of columnists, to give "balance," a tendentious editorial page, prevailingly Republican, compete for space with social news and advertisements of supermarket specials. My first hope, I thought, of getting any real coverage would be when I finally reached an area served by the Los Angeles *Times*, a pro-Administration paper with fair and comprehensive news columns. But not at all. In every city I arrived at, the local papers were full of Watergate; regardless of their politics and of pressure, if any, from their advertisers, they were keeping their readers in touch with the most minor episodes in this fantastic crime serial.

Television, with its half-hour nightly news summary larded with commercials and rather fatty comment, was not up to the job of telling the tale (this was before the Ervin Committee had started its hearings), and the newspapers, rising to the emergency, had come into their own, as though Marshall McLuhan had never been thought of and we were back in the Gutenberg Galaxy. Television let us see Nixon give his April 30 speech, flanked by a bust of Abraham Lincoln and photographs of his family; heavily made up, he announced the resignations of those fine public servants Haldeman and Ehrlichman and seemed to be coaxing a tear that refused to drop. This ought to have been a television natural, like the Checkers speech, but television was the wrong medium for a public suddenly hungry for facts, not images and stage props, and the speech failed to satisfy. Meanwhile newspaper sales must have been jumping all over the country. People were buying not one but two or even three, plus *Time* and *Newsweek*. On airplanes I watched the silent majority, vociferous as usual, turn first to the news pages and *then* to the sports pages as if with a single motion.

Nixon's speech failed, not because he was uneasy, like a bad actor—this has always been so—but because it was irrelevant. The country wanted information, and Nixon was incapable—genuinely, I think—of understanding that. Aside from the fact that his interest was in concealment rather than in laying bare, he was unable to see that elocution, an appearance of confidentiality, was not a substitute for information, having long ago lost the power, probably, to distinguish between the two. He may well have been mystified by his speech's lack of success: he was appealing for trust, as he had so often before—why wasn't it work-

4

ing? He could not grasp that Watergate had quickened in his listeners an old appetite for narrative, for the unfolding of a plot, and to him this was something new and inexplicable, at least in the sphere of public affairs. Well, he was not only firing Dean but sacrificing Haldeman and Ehrlichman and Attorney General Kleindienst to that appetite and going before the cameras to do it: shouldn't that close the subject? But the announcement of four dismissals (three disguised as uncoerced resignations) did not answer public questions but merely raised new ones. With the nation's eyes on him, wasn't he going to tell *why* those men were going? No; he evidently did not see the necessity. Facts, which the nation was asking for, were to him foreign objects which he had somehow recently bumped up against without comprehending their nature. He relied on television, his familiar instrument, to allow him to glide past them with a straightforward air, when he would have done better to stay out of view and give a curt hand-out to the press he so mistrusted.

Nixon is a television creation, a sort of gesturing phantom, uncomfortable in the old-fashioned world of printer's type, where assertions can be checked and verified. His aversion to the press is understandable, and it is not an accident that the Watergate story, in its early chapters, lent itself not to the fugitive images of television but to durable columns of closely set newsprint. Printer's ink and domestic liberty have an old association. Whereas television, being a mass medium, can be controlled and manipulated, total control of the printed word, as has been demonstrated in the Soviet Union, seems to be all but impossible. If newspapers are censored or suppressed, broadsides and leaflets can still circulate, passing from hand to hand. The revival of the U.S. press under Nixon is an essential part of the Watergate phenomenon, like the judiciary's declaration of independence—Judge Sirica.

Essential as both cause and effect. Not only did two talented young reporters, Woodward and Bernstein of the Washington *Post,* precipitate the facts of the June break-in that had remained for months in a murky suspended solution; newspapers became indispensable to the nation's understanding of Watergate. The enormous and continually widening cast of characters, the complicated, often obscure and difficult plot made cross-reference obligatory for anybody who wanted to be "in" on the fascinating event. In American houses, whole Watergate libraries of old newspapers and news magazines have been accumulating, like the bundles we used to save up for our school paper drives when I was a girl. Someday all this paper may be recycled, but meanwhile, as the investigation continues, on a diversity of fronts, with grand juries sitting in Washington, New York, Florida, California, and Senate and House committees, as well as the Special Prosecutor, taking pertinent testimony, the record grows more brain-taxing. There are so many numbers in it, crucial dates to be held in the head and arithmetic involving various sums of money deposited in and withdrawn from various safes and bank accounts, turned into cashiers' checks and then back into cash, "laundered" in Mexico, borrowed, repaid, occasionally returned to the donor or passed, no questions asked, to "a man named Tony."

There are moments when one feels that only a computer could digest the daily input of Watergate scandal. And yet the American people have mastered Watergate; they are able to keep it all straight, even the ITT sub-plot of Dita Beard and Howard Hunt in a red wig and the Vesco interlude. What a treat to find Americans who are not professional intellectuals engrossed in what is a decidedly intellectual study, requiring feats of memory, concentration, orderly procedure. Housewives, they say, now that Senator Ervin's hearings are eating up four hours a day of TV time, complain that they miss their soap operas. If true, this is not surprising. It would be a weird country indeed in which housewives or any group trying to do semi-skilled labor would acquiescently set the dial to a public-affairs program demanding undivided attention and in which the human interest, though in some cases lively, is flickering. Or minimal, as in this week's testimony by former Secretary of Commerce Maurice Stans, a silver-haired, sideburned super-accountant and magic fund-raiser, who gave a day-and-a-half-long demonstration of the athletics of evasion, showing himself very fit for a man of his age—middle sixties—but inviting more wonder than sympathy.

Actually, it is surprising how faithfully and closely these televised hearings are followed; for those who missed the daytime sessions, there is an evening rerun on educational TV, starting at eight (Eastern Daylight Time) and lasting till after midnight, and people all over the country, according to their time zones, adjust their dinner hour and their bedtime to watch it. One old lady in Los Angeles, her daughter told me, has changed her whole schedule, including visits to the hairdresser and card games, to fit the Ervin hearings. Here television shows its real usefulness, that of reproducing an event in its entirety, as it does with sports and political conventions. Yet without the supplement of the daily newspaper and the weekly news magazines, it is doubtful whether the public would have been up to the televised spectacle. For those unable to watch (*e.g.*, taxi drivers) there is the radio, which carries the hearings throughout the day: a customer getting into a cab will ask who is doing the questioning; "Dash," says the driver, or "Baker," turning up the volume.

The best, though, is to see the spectacle in the flesh, in the marble-pillared Senate Caucus Room, rather shabby, and not as commodious as one would expect. A good part of the interest is in the crowd, standing three and sometimes four deep against the back wall or seated, the luckier ones, in the few roped-off rows of chairs. Young people predominate, but there are all ages and kinds: teen-agers, small children (I have not yet seen a baby), priests, old women in aluminum walkers, one or two mad people in crazed costumes. There is almost continuous movement in and out of the room, reminding one of the Sistine Chapel. Here, however, there are no guides; uniformed, gun-wearing cops act as custodians of senatorial dignity and direct the flow of human traffic. And though some of these massed spectators, including foreigners, must be tourists visiting the capital, they do not act like tourists. Everybody is serious, almost grave. Not respectful exactly but intent, as though they were a self-elected jury, especially the younger ones, come to judge for themselves.

They have obviously been following the hearings on television and need no introduction to the principal figures. Some pretty Southern women I talked to had come all the way from Louisville, Kentucky, to spend two days in the Caucus Room; their senator had got them seats. They knew more about the cast of characters than I did, though I had been boning up. "We watch it evvra night." At home, that is. The same with some students in cut-off jeans down from Boston. They had CREEP's financing at their fingertips and interpreted for me a bit.

Compared with them, I was an amateur, a real greenhorn. Watergate has been a great equalizer. It has cut across class lines, party lines, intellectual lines. Except for a small group of people, mostly moneyed, in my experience, who claim to be bored to death by all the coverage, everybody has been fully participating, and nobody, in principle, given the equality of opportunity available, is more of an expert than the next person. It was not so with Vietnam, where a sophisticated group was almost over-informed, while the rest of the population remained ignorant or indifferent. You get the impression that those intent spectators in the Senate Caucus Room are the delegates of a much larger assembly that is watching and judging in homes, offices, campuses, factories. This is a trial, all right, as Nixon's defenders complain, but not by the Senate panel, which as it takes testimony, asks or fails to ask questions, is being judged too.

With his white fluffy celebrity sideburns, small, well-cut features, smart suit accessorized with tie-clasp and cuff-

links bearing the presidential seal, Maurice Stans resembled a successful actor, a combination of Claude Rains
in *Caesar and Cleopatra* and Claude Dauphin. He also had
something of a courtly, highly paid, dignified Park Avenue
doctor. He entered the hearing-room with an erect bearing,
a stately leisured pace, accompanied by his court of three
lawyers, like interns following the chief during a ward visit.
The effect throughout his smooth-flowing testimony was of
a busy man conferring a favor, glad to take time to en-
lighten the senators on technical matters regarding the dis-
position of funds that were beyond their sphere of com-
petence. It was as though the realities—that he was under
indictment in New York for perjury and obstruction of justice and was appearing here under duress, in answer to a
subpoena—had been sublimely transcended, and several of
the senators seemed to join him in the illusion. When he
took his leave, on a note of sudden oratorical pathos ("Give
me back my good name!"), you almost thought they were
going to lean forward and ask him for his autograph.

Not astute old Senator Ervin, however, an actor in his
own right, with a far wider range, virtually Shakespearean,
and showing the Bard's own fondness for character parts
and honest common-sense rustics. In these hearings, Senator
Ervin represents the humble, "low" reality principle and
has clearly chosen to do so, which is why the audience loves
him. His common sense was outraged by Stans's continued
professions of having known nothing, seen nothing, done
nothing, above all *thought* nothing about the sums of money
passing sometimes through his secretary's safe, sometimes
through a network of bank accounts, to the Watergate con-

spirators. Stans said he only knew what he read in the newspapers, and unlike the ordinary newspaper reader, despite his skill in accountancy, he never tried, it seems, to put two and two together.

When Kalmbach, Nixon's lawyer, came to him on June 23 to ask if he could give him, quick, $75,000 for an urgent unspecified purpose of interest to an unnamed "high authority," it never *occurred* to Stans that there could be any connection with the five men caught in the Watergate early in the morning of June 17 or with the arrest, reported the next day in the press, of their leader, McCord, an operative on Stans's payroll. Like everybody else in the country, Stans now knows that the $75,000 was needed to buy the arrested men's silence ("pay their legal fees," in his terminology), but at the time he just handed the cash to Kalmbach without a question in his mind: "He was a man of the highest integrity." As though the only question that *might* have insinuated itself was whether Kalmbach was planning to steal the seventy-five grand. A clash between this bland ectoplasmic creature and Senator Ervin was bound to come, for natural reason could stand no more, and when it did, it was like a meeting between an astral body and a hard crusty earth object. "I am an old country lawyer," Ervin began, plaintive-voiced, and the audience burst out laughing and clapping before he could complete the sentence.

The next witness, Jeb Stuart Magruder (romantically named after the Confederate cavalry general), was a refreshing change from the fluent, labile Stans. At least at the start. Candid, pink-cheeked, blue-eyed, with horrible diction that seemed to guarantee his authenticity, he was contrite for his "errors" and determined to prove it by making a full confession and implicating others, though not beyond the extent that was "fair." This extent, it soon appeared, stopped just short of Haldeman and hesitated around Stans. Those who were expecting him to nail Stans (as leaks had promised he would) were in for a disappointment. In private session, he had told the Committee that Stans had learned from John Mitchell on June 24 the "basic details" about Watergate; now, in the witness chair just vacated by Stans, he was no longer sure how much Mitchell and he had said to the fund-raiser straight out and how much they had left to inference. Now his "best recollection" was that they "didn't go into specifics" that day. In short, by modifying his testimony, he accommodated it to Stans's. Perhaps, having heard Stans, he was only trying to be fair.

Fairness allowed the guilt of Mitchell himself, of John Dean, Robert Mardian (a former assistant attorney general), Fred LaRue (Mitchell's campaign assistant), Gordon Strachan (Haldeman's aide). It assigned smaller portions of blame to Hugh Sloan, Jr., and to Herbert Porter, who had already admitted perjury in the cover-up, and skirted Ehrlichman, who was not in the witness's command chain.

The planning and execution of the cover-up were described in some detail, as well as the steps by which Mitchell had arrived at approval of the Watergate break-in. A sub-project—the burglary, proposed by Mitchell or Dean (Magruder forgot which), of Hank Greenspun's safe in Las Vegas, supposedly to get material damaging to Muskie, at that point the Democratic front-runner—was assigned to Liddy to "review." On Watergate, it had taken Mitchell three meetings to make up his mind to say yes to Liddy or, as Magruder put it, "there was a delay in the decision-making process" because of "the ITT business," which was weighing heavy on the Attorney General's mind. He had to put the cover on that before he could turn his full attention to burglarizing the Democratic National Committee headquarters.

Magruder's zeal to be fair in the witness's seat was perhaps a genuine part of the cliché around which he was building a fresh, contrite personality. He lost no opportunity to put in a good word for those he was implicating, to tell how it had looked to them—and to himself—almost funny, in a way. A crazy guy like Liddy; you could hardly take him seriously. Whenever possible, he sought to give his former employers a break: perhaps Mr. Haldeman never saw the reports Mr. Strachan should have been passing on to him—"You'll have to ask Mr. Strachan, sir." It is being widely reported that Magruder incriminated Haldeman, but whenever he came near doing so he ran hastily in the opposite direction. The only clearly damaging testimony he gave about Haldeman was that in January of this year, some time before the Inaugural, he had gone to Haldeman and told him the truth about Watergate and the cover-up. "I thought probably that this was maybe becoming scapegoat time and maybe I was going to be the scapegoat, and I went to Mr. Haldeman and I said I just want you to know that this whole Watergate situation and the other activities was a concerted effort by a number of people, and so I went through literally a monologue on what had occurred. This was my first discussion with Mr. Haldeman where I laid out the true facts." Now the public might ask why, if Haldeman learned these facts from Magruder in January, he did not at once inform Nixon, but in the Watergate black book this omission would be a relatively minor sin, and the whole burden of Magruder's artless account was to suggest Haldeman's complete ignorance, up to then, of both the break-in and the cover-up.

An eagerness to exculpate his superiors or to mitigate their guilt was modestly evident throughout Magruder's testimony. Knowing the White House methods as he did, from the inside, he was convinced, he said, that no word of the planned break-in had ever got to the President. As for Mitchell, he had and has "great respect for him." "A wonderful leader." And "I respected Mr. Haldeman tremendously. I still do. A very fine man." He emphasized Mitchell's reluctance to approve the Liddy plan, even in its third and scaled-down version: "I think I can honestly say that no one was particularly overwhelmed with the project." Again, "But it was a reluctant decision. I think that is important to note. It was not one that anyone was overwhelmed with at all." And Haldeman's June 18 telephone call from Key Biscayne to Magruder in Beverly Hills to demand "What happened?" could mean "What went wrong?" but not necessarily. Magruder was not going to pronounce on what Mr. Haldeman had meant by the question; that would be out of place.

All this loving charity and forbearance, this unwillingness to judge or censure may represent a virtuous effort to live up to his own simplistic picture of a new, reformed, chastened Magruder. References to the prodigal son keep cropping up in his talks with interviewers. He told the Senate Committee that he expected to come out of the Watergate ordeal a better man: "I am not going to lay down and die because of it."

Yet it was possible to suspect, listening to him, that he was being not so much "sincere"—as Senator Weicker, much affected, told him—as extremely careful. It might be that his testimony was as carefully groomed and combed as his hair, that he had been urged or had urged himself to set a limit on his admissions and correct previous admissions that had overstepped it. A pattern could be seen: on one side of the line of demarcation were himself, Mitchell, Dean, Mardian, LaRue, and the smaller fry, already too fatally compromised not to be jettisoned; on the other, Nixon, Haldeman, and Ehrlichman, and somewhere on the border, Stans. All of this second group could still be safe if the team tightened up and played wise ball.

It had been evident that Stans, considering himself a team-player, was going to divulge nothing, despite overwhelming evidence that he knew a great deal, and it slowly became evident that Magruder, too, still considered himself a team-player, despite all he had divulged, being in a tight spot and needing immunity. That motive would be understandable to the Nixon team, and Magruder may hope to be forgiven by it, to receive a form of "executive clemency" and be taken back into the fold. In the case of this particular well-shorn lamb, there are more ways than one of reading the prodigal son parable.

Plainly Jeb Stuart Magruder, whether exiled from the Nixon fold or not, remains an unreconstructed right-winger. In accounting for Watergate, he sought understanding for the "psychology" that prevailed in the White House, and that psychology, in turn, he blamed on radicals and dissenters, like his old teacher, the Reverend William Sloane Coffin, under whom he once took a course in Ethics at Williams College. One saw that he felt that Coffin, "still a close friend of mine," had betrayed him and Ethics by coming down to Washington to take part in anti-war demonstrations, by encouraging illegal acts like draft-card burning and threatening in a speech to "shut down" Washington, *i.e.*, to try to paralyze traffic. Magruder now knows, he told the senators, that he should not have let his "resentment and frustration" over the illegal activities of anti-war groups lead *him* into illegality. "Two wrongs don't make a right," he has concluded. In other words, he and Coffin are fellow-sinners (though he himself has since seen the light), a pair of black sheep. He still cannot discern a difference between open civil disobedience with its long American tradition going back to the Boston Tea Party and the purely expedient covert criminality of Watergate and its sequel. Senator Ervin, a civil-libertarian, pulled him up sharp. "Dr. Coffin was just *demonstratin'*, wasn't he?" Magruder did not catch the point. Suddenly, for the first time, his soft dimpled features toughened. His jaw thrust forward aggressively, and he muttered that anti-war activities had been destroying the President's peace initiative. For a young man in that sullen state of mind, close to moral idiocy, there is nowhere to go but back on the team.

Notes
of a
Watergate
Resident

June 24, 1973

This has been the week of the so-called Brezhnev recess. Senator Ervin's panel, in order not to embarrass Nixon before his Soviet guest, voted to suspend the Watergate hearings during the state visit. Otherwise we might have had the treat of seeing the First Secretary of the party among the foreign spectators in the Senate Caucus Room, seated in the first row with his translator and his body guards while John Dean testified to whatever he is going to testify—despite leaks, no one yet can be sure. A functionary from the State Department (or maybe General Haig?) could have briefed the Brezhnev party on the curious and to them perhaps Swiftian workings of democracy. Instead, Washington has been waiting irritably for Brezhnev to go home, so that traffic can be restored to normal and Dean can at last be heard. On the personal side, I ought to be grateful for the postponement. For the first time since I have been here, I have leisure to look around at the physical setting of the Watergate break-in and to think a little about the moral setting or "ecology" out of which it emerged.

I get an appreciative chuckle whenever I tell people I am staying at the Watergate Hotel. Even before the break-in, the ten-acre aggregate comprising three co-operatives, the hotel, and two office buildings began to tickle the public fancy because the Mitchells lived here—in the co-operative

known as Watergate East—at the time when Martha, looking out of the window of her husband's office downtown at
the Justice Department, watched "the very liberal Com-
munists, the worst kind" demonstrating in the street below.

Now the Mitchell tenure here and that of Maurice Stans
are only vaguely recalled; what tourists come to look at
and be photographed in front of are the office building,
where the Democratic National Committee had its headquarters on the sixth floor, and the more plebeian red-
roofed Howard Johnson Motor Lodge, opposite, where the
listening-post of the wire-tappers was situated. Tourists also
roam through the hotel lobby, buy Watergate joke material,
including bugs, at the newsstand, and take a peep at the
Watergate Terrace Restaurant overlooking the outdoor
swimming pool (restricted to co-operative residents; there
is an indoor swimming pool, with sauna, for hotel guests),
where McCord and his men are supposed to have had a
lobster dinner before the break-in.

As the hotel literature puts it, "The Watergate Complex,
one of the most distinctive private real estate developments
in the nation, offers a way of life that is complete in every
respect . . . for you, the visitor, as well as for those who
reside and/or work in this pace-setting community." Designed by an Italian architect, the whole complex, with the
exception of the office buildings, bristles with rows of stony
teeth, which are a sort of coping around the balconies opening off nearly every room. The impression is of an updated
medieval fortress, quite extensive, and between Watergate
East and Watergate South there is what looks like a Bridge
of Sighs, topped by an American flag. Those uniform gray-

white teeth projecting from the curious swollen shapes, elliptical, wedge-like, semi-circular, of the building units, suggest a sea animal—a whale, somebody said, but also something sharkish. To assure privacy, balconies are separated from each other by what seem to be cement fins. Maybe the marine imagery is meant to be in harmony with the Potomac setting. The teeth, on close inspection, turn out to be made of tiny stones pressed into cement, giving a scaly effect.

Even though it is summer and not always too hot, almost nobody appears on the balconies, which are the main architectural feature; empty garden furniture stares out from them on the landscaped grounds. Once I saw a single figure, a fat woman in a pink wrapper, wander ghost-like behind her toothy parapet. Yet at some point in time, as the Ervin Committee witnesses express it, somebody must have used *my* balcony, for when I arrived, ten days ago, two empty beer cans (Budweiser) were lying there; this morning, finally, they were gone—the window-washer had come by. On a few of the co-operative balconies, there are some ill-tended, long-suffering flowering plants. The cells of this "community" are not neighborly; no voices call across the outdoor expanse, and the rooms are effectively sound-proofed.

The sense of being in a high-security castellated fort or series of forts is added to by lower-level passages, known as Malls, which constitute a labyrinth. The whole place, in fact, is a maze, marked here and there by highly misleading signs directing you to *"Les Champs,"* "Mall," "Restaurant," "Arcade." When you try to follow them, you either go round in circles or end up against a blank, no-entry wall. It is as if there were a war on, and the red, green, and blue directional arrows had been turned to point the wrong way in order to confuse the enemy expected to invade at sunrise. Every day, so far, I have got lost in this eerie complex, hoping to find an Espresso bar that was rumored to exist somewhere in the vicinity of *"Les Champs."* Once I found myself in "Peacock Alley," and another time standing on the verge of the forbidden swimming pool. Yesterday, though, I reached the goal, following the instructions of a porter: "You just keep goin' around."

This Kafkian quest for the Espresso bar had an economic motive. I was comparison-shopping the breakfasts available. The People's Drugstore, in a "popular" region of the Mall near the hotel, is the cheapest, offering fruit juice, toasted English muffin, grape jelly, and coffee for sixty cents; the Howard Johnson, across from the famed office building, is the best value, giving you the same but with a better muffin and a *choice* of grape jelly or marmalade for eighty cents; the hotel Terrace Restaurant calls this—with an inferior muffin but more copious marmalade—a Continental breakfast and charges two dollars and fifty cents. The Espresso bar, which doubles as a hot-dog stand, does not serve breakfast, it turns out, but is a fairly good value for a sandwich- or salad-and-coffee lunch. It too has a "popular" clientele, and it was there I heard a young girl, yesterday, say to her friend, "Senator Ervin? I heard him on the radio. He's real sharp."

The main attraction, though, of the Watergate complex was intended, evidently, to be the shopping, ranging from low-cost, lower-level (the People's Drugstore and a Safeway, where Senator Brooke, they say, can be seen with a shopping bag full of groceries), to unarmed robbery in *"Les Champs."* There are Pierre Cardin, Gucci, Yves St. Laurent, Enzo Boutique for men, located in the "exclusive" end, and Saks and more moderate shoe and dress shops along the arcade. But you can buy almost any kind of goods and services, short of guns or a suit of armor, in these labyrinthine ways: wigs, pottery and china, jewelry, antiques, Uruguayan handicrafts, patchwork, Swedish everything, Oriental everything, flowers, liquor (including Watergate brands of scotch and bourbon, now much in demand by souvenir hunters), insurance, air tickets and hotel reservations. In the Mall, there are an optician and a U.S. post office; a bookstore, the Savile, has gone out of business and a cheese shop is moving into the space. On the street level there are a bank and a building-and-loan association. As the hotel flyer indicates, the idea has been to make Watergate as nearly as possible self-sustaining. As though it were under siege.

This, I suppose, is the Watergate mentality, in a more general sense: a compound of money, the isolation or insulation it can buy, and fear. Though conceived as a cosmopolitan center, the result is rather pathetically suburban and middle-American. What it boils down to is not very different from any of the so-called shopping malls along U.S. highways. Except that they can usually support at least a paperback bookstore.

The hotel employment policy seems to be somehow meaningful and to imply a curious notion of classification, like that distinguishing the Malls from the Arcade and *"Les Champs."* Downstairs, in front, the help is mainly Spanish-speaking—one imagines a staff of brown-uniformed Cuban defectors, potential recruits for CREEP and the CIA. In the Terrace Restaurant, again Spanish-speaking, but in red uniforms and with a few Southeast Asians and East Europeans added—more CIA material? Upstairs, the chambermaids and maintenance men, who constitute the core of the hotel invisible from below, are nearly all black; I think of Ralph Ellison and his invisible man. Probably there is a key to employment policy here that eludes me; maybe it is artistic—a matter of subtle color blends and contrasts, designed to please the eye.

A French friend, in town for a picture story on the hearings, says he thinks that the Americans are using Watergate to cleanse themselves of guilt for Vietnam. As he says this, a light goes on in my mind. Yes, he is right; if it had not been for Vietnam, the scandal of the break-in might have soon dropped from notice like previous scandals—a tempest in a teapot.

I had assumed it was just luck, a happy coincidence of independent factors—the zeal of the Washington *Post* in tracking down the story, Judge Sirica's determination to be told the truth, the early leaks coming from the Justice Department and the FBI—that had brought about disclosure and led to what is now spoken of as a turning point in the nation's history or at least of Richard Nixon's place in it. None of these factors singly would have sufficed, but all of them converging, plus Senator Ervin, did it, and many editorialists took pride in this as showing that the American system—the judiciary, the press, the Congress—worked to curb the arrogant power of the executive. No doubt this is true (though we have not yet seen the end), but without another factor—Vietnam—the pursuit of truth, I now feel, might have been less vigorous and public interest slight.

Because of Vietnam, the country suddenly wants to be *"clean,"* as my French friend said. Watergate is the scrubbing brush, sometimes painful to the skin, since it is not easy on the national touchiness to have all those cosmetics scrubbed away. Watergate hurts many simple patriots, to the point where they don't want to hear about it. This is understandable when you think of Nixon's "landslide"—the millions of voters who must to some degree have identified themselves with the image he presented on the TV screen. What is surprising is the turnabout: the vast numbers that now watch the rapid erosion of that image without too much complaint. Most of those viewers participated with Richard Nixon and with LBJ before him in the crime of Vietnam.

It is worth examining the fact that those most prominent now in the pursuit of truth about Watergate (*i.e.*, about the character-potentialities of the President; what may he still be capable of?) were not, to say the least, among the leading opponents of the war in Vietnam. I do not know Judge Sirica's voting record but I do not recall seeing his name on any peace manifesto; the same for Archibald Cox. Of the senators on the Ervin Committee I wonder how many took a stand against the war. Well, on the McGovern-Hatfield amendment cutting off funds for Indochina after December 31, 1971—scarcely the acid test—two, Montoya and Inouye, voted Yes. We know the position of Goldwater, who is now calling for the truth, and I believe he means it. Judge Sirica, most of the senators of the Committee, and Goldwater must be fairly representative of that almost consistent majority that answered "Approve" when asked by pollsters for their opinion of U.S. policy in Vietnam.

The innocent in that crime, if anybody can be considered so, *i.e.*, the liberals and radicals who spoke out and demonstrated, have been taking rather a back seat in the Watergate investigation. As far as the Congress goes, this is being ascribed to a Democratic party strategy of letting the Republicans carry the ball, to avoid giving any appearance of narrow partisanship: let his own party call for Nixon's impeachment or go to him and demand that he resign. No doubt that strategy is operating, but there is something deeper involved that has compelled conservatives of both parties to play leading roles in the investigation and compels ordinary lifelong Republicans to demand the truth almost more loudly than the rest of us—possibly because they had had no suspicion of it before.

One can say that Watergate is a good test to determine who is really a conservative and who just pretends to be: Goldwater passes the test; Senator Ervin passes with honors; Agnew fails; William Buckley gets a D. But are there, then, as many true conservatives in the country as poll results on Watergate (58 per cent think Nixon was in on it, after if not before) by this criterion would seem to show? I wonder, having found it difficult in my private, pre-Watergate experience to meet more than one or two, though I have gone out with a Diogenes lantern.

It might be safer to conclude that 58 per cent of the nation still has some common sense left and can be trusted to serve on a jury. But I will go further and say that a considerable per cent of that per cent (reducing the figure to allow for those who think Nixon guilty but regard it as "just politics," who are in other words a-political and don't care) has a conscience. On which Vietnam has weighed. Despite all rationalization. Napalm, defoliants, area bombing, Lazy Dogs, anti-personnel missiles, these means to achieve an end presumed to be virtuous have cost this country much secret pain.

Watergate too has been justified before the Senate Committee as a means to achieve a similar though not identical end: the defeat of subversion through the re-election of Nixon. Watergate too is advanced technology enlisted in the service of patriotism. Of course the means of Watergate are much less repellent than napalm and cluster bombs. Wire-tapping doesn't "hurt anybody." That may be why the emerging truth of Watergate could be faced day after day by such a large part of the U.S. population. It did not seem, at the beginning, too heavy a load for the national conscience to shoulder, and confession would have been good for the White House collective soul. Yet confession did not come; Nixon did not make "a clean breast" in his much awaited April 30 television appearance. He sacrificed Haldeman, Ehrlichman, Kleindienst, Dean to the gods of retribution but failed to appease them. The guilty secrets

27

remained unadmitted and in fact increased and multiplied, or, rather, first suspicion, then knowledge of them did.

It was no longer just the little sin of wire-tapping but lying, perjury, bribery, burglary, obstruction of justice, misuse of funds, fraud, extortion, forgery. The discovered guilt spread till it embraced nearly every common crime short of rape and murder. Suspicion fell heavily on Agnew's fund-raising dinner and reached out to San Clemente to touch not only the shrouded financing of the purchase but Nixon's office chair, his lamp, his septic tank, bought with public money, to enhance his security and aid him in the transaction of the national business. Certainly this kind of petty profit-taking—charging off personal expenses to the company—is S.O.P. among certain categories of American businessmen, and Nixon may have been incapable of distinguishing the nation from a company of which he was chairman of the board.

It is quite likely that he was unaware of any wrongdoing in many of the shady operations that have come to light: wire-tapping of rival firms is common in business, and donations to public officials are as much taken for granted as fixing a parking ticket. Except in the matters of burglary and subornation of perjury, he and his aides did not make any great departure from the prevailing business ethic. Startled by the public outcry, he may have waked up to the existence of another world, with other standards than those he and his associates were accustomed to.

In any case, unable to face the louder and louder music, he found no way of "containing" the Watergate scandal. Meanwhile every fresh disclosure, far from exhausting the public capacity for shock, whetted the appetite for more and worse revelations, as if the desire for truth was unslakable, had no limits, although in normal circumstances this is seldom the case: "Don't tell me any more" is a common plea, except in crises of sexual jealousy.

The public's ability to absorb more shocks than it was originally prepared for can be explained by the residue of guilt left over from Vietnam, guilt unadmitted by the majority and therefore all the more in need of relief. There has been much talk about atonement in the Senate Committee's proceedings, some of it hypocritical on the part of both senators and witnesses. Senator Baker's insistent questions about motive suggest that he is playing a TV role of spiritual surgeon and counselor, and only once, I feel, did his pious probing elicit a truthful answer; when Herbert Porter told him, "I did not do it [perjury] for money . . . for power . . . for position. My vanity was appealed to. They said I was talked about in high councils . . . that I was an honest man."

Porter said he had recognized, looking back, a weakness in himself he had not been conscious of. This simple, direct, and rather touching answer, however, did not seem to be what Senator Baker had been after when he talked musingly of "atonement"; if I recall right, he quickly dropped the subject. As for Jeb Stuart Magruder, I myself was less saddened by the evidence that Williams College had been unable to teach him Ethics (it would have been a tough job) than by the grammar it had left him with: "Mitchell told he and I" would be a fair sample. The senators' readiness to be moved and edified by Magruder's repentant posture led them to overlook the fact that he did not admit to a single weakness or character flaw, but only to "mistakes." Mistakes made from an excess of good motives, naturally. The idea that these hearings ought to be morally *improving* (*i.e.*, ought to show a profit) made most of the senators easy marks for Magruder.

Yet behind all the facile moralizing, I think, there is some notion of a genuine need for atonement and purification. Obviously, identification of the guilty in Watergate and associated crimes will not "make up" for Vietnam or wash it away, but I do not blame anybody for the wish and even think it a good thing. You cannot undo Vietnam, but that is true of most offenses, certainly all those involving murder, where no restitution is possible. You can't bring back the dead, and with many other wrongs, when contrition arrives, it is generally too late.

Atonement is directed not toward the victims but toward the crime, that is, toward the injury inflicted by the crime— on God or on the fragile social tissue holding living beings together. Some degree of repair here is possible, or at least the attempt is salutary and may benefit the criminal, if nobody else. Ever since my mind and emotions became centered on Vietnam, I have been thinking about the problem of purgation and atonement. Perhaps this is due, a little, to living in France throughout this period, where so many of the early churches, abbeys, and hospitals you visit are memorials of some horrible blood crime committed by a high-placed person, king, duke, or noble. This is particularly true of Normandy and the Plantagenet country, where there was an unusual degree of violence. These religious buildings were blood money exacted by God, *i.e.*, by the conscience, never by the Church. In other words, they were not a punishment but a self-punishment and served a double purpose: of symbolically washing away the blood the murderer had shed and of making that blood, so to speak, indelible, crying out to Heaven for as long as the abbey-church or Old Men's Hospice would stand.

Modern people, by contrast, have no way of dealing with guilt, which is probably why they so seldom acknowledge it. I used to wonder about public men like McNamara, who, apparently seeing the error of his ways, left LBJ's government. When anybody has done anything as bad as what they did, there ought to be some possibility of redemption. McNamara, in my opinion, would have been better off had he retired to a monastery rather than to the World Bank. McGeorge Bundy, if in any way penitent, scarcely demonstrated it by his switch to the Ford Foundation. The old recourse of philanthropy used by big-scale public sinners like Carnegie, Frick, and Rockefeller to signify, if not atonement, repayment of a slight debt to humanity is now just another tax write-off. Reparations are paid, if at all, by governments, never by an individual war criminal.

It is hard to see Nixon abdicating like Charles V to seek peace in a little house attached to a monastery or its Quakerish equivalent, but with LBJ one could just barely picture some Texan Thebaid, where he might have dotted the land with anchorites' cells for himself and his cronies. If the various Watergate inquiries, trials, civil suits, and grand jury hearings are, as I feel, steps toward purgation, cathartic efforts, on the part of the country as a whole, direct expiation is being suggested, though, only to those pale or pink-faced young men, wearing earnest glasses, who have appeared before the Ervin Committee. It is as if they were expected, through type casting, like little oblates, to expiate all the nation's sins against its own conception of itself. "Mr. Porter," declared Senator Ervin, "you give the appearance of a man who was brought up in a good home." "Yes, Senator, I was." The thought, certainly, would not occur to anybody about John Mitchell, who looks as if he were brought up in a reformatory. The burden of repentance is being offered to the *young* Republicans or to those among them, like Porter and Hugh Sloan, who have a quality of innocence.

Yet what are they supposed to do, exactly, to redeem themselves and their country? This is not clear. The free admission of wrongdoing is a first step, but where are they meant to go from there? They have been trained in American business life, and that, presumably, is what they will return to, as they try to "reinstate themselves" in society. But the society itself is corrupted, as their testimony before the Senate interrogators demonstrates. They do not belong in jail, but the good home of which Senator Ervin spoke—and we all knew what he meant—is situated almost in another century.

Metaphorically speaking, it is America, the "old" parental America. Senator Ervin still believes in it and has his eleven-year-old yellow-haired grandson acting as a Senate page-boy in the Caucus Room to offer as proof. This house, he feels, with a little elbow-grease can be cleaned and restored to at least a semi-pristine condition. That is why he is stubbornly convinced that the hearings will arrive at their destination—the truth. "But if it doesn't come out that way?" I said to him. "If they fail? Just take it as a hypothesis." "I refuse to entertain the thought" was his answer, as though the thought was a felon seeking entry into his mental premises. He is becoming a folk hero because of that stout, old-fashioned attitude. I hope he is right, but if he is right and nothing then happens—a strong possibility —then we are worse off than we were before. If we know, that is, and don't act, can find no frame for action, Nixon and his sly firm, *knowing* that *we* know and won't do anything, will have nothing more to fear.

The Wagons Are Drawn Up Around the White House

June 30, 1973

Tuesday afternoon, during one of the recesses, at the open
door of the Caucus Room I noticed an elderly bald-fronted
man with a long white Tolstoyan beard and long reddish-
white curling Doukhoborish locks. He was dressed in what
looked like an airy ample jump suit, pale yellow with short
sleeves and made of some lawn-like material recalling old-
fashioned BVDs. His stout figure in that floating garment
gave an appearance of bustle. As I learned later, he had
been polling the spectators, who by now were standing five
deep against the back wall. He had picked out twelve at
random to constitute a jury and decide on the question: is
John Dean telling the truth? Or, framed another way: is
Nixon guilty?

They had voted unanimously Yes, and two other spectators had begged to have their votes counted: "Make it
fourteen." When the hearings broke up, I found myself
sharing a cab with this sandy, eccentric character, who took
up quite a lot of room—cab-sharing at rush hours is a
Washington custom, and there were four of us, including
two Minneapolis newsmen. He was going to the airport, having stopped off for the day at the hearings on his way home
from Montreal, where he had been "on a pastoral mission."
That was to the U.S. deserters and resisters in Canada—
very Tolstoyan. Though he looked more like the prophet
Elijah than like a contemporary pastor, he was a Methodist

minister and represented the Southern Council of Church-
men. He had been hoping Nixon was innocent—a proof of
Christian charity—despite a long-standing dislike of the
man. He told me he feared that his jury might have been a
little bit "selective": Nixon's friends, he guessed, would
stay away from the Senate Caucus Room. I agreed. Just
before I got out of the cab, at the Watergate Hotel, he
polled the driver, a young black: "Do you think he's
guilty?" "No, sir, I don't think he's guilty." Pause, high
laugh. "I *know* it. Isn't no way he couldn't know what was
going on."

Next day, the French photographer I was walking with
across a park behind the Senate Office Building was halted
and polled by a young man with a Burgundy-red beard and
dressed in an electric-blue nylon get-up that looked as if it
had come straight from planetary space. He had been
taking samplings that morning in the Caucus Room while
Senator Gurney of Florida, a Nixonite with a bronze-gray
marcel wave, was grilling the witness with sarcastic demands about his honeymoon, the state of his bank account,
how he had been obliged to leave a law firm for reasons
having to do with the ethics of obtaining a TV license. The
result of this poll was the same, though the spaced-out
young man hadn't hit on the concept of twelve good men
and true and the spectators he had asked thought Dean
was telling the truth but probably didn't want to. Doubtless
this sample was younger and, not content with judging his
testimony, wanted to judge the man too.

Very American, I suppose—natural rough justice. But

how else do you form an opinion as to whether somebody is lying or not? Nixon has told his side on carefully stage-managed television but shrinks from the open forum. As Senator Ervin said, discussing some of the leaks tending to discredit Dean in advance: "There isn't anybody that can decide on the credibility of a witness till they listen to him give his testimony." The notion that only a pillar of the community can be trusted to tell the truth under oath (Hugh Scott, the Republican Senate leader, brushed off Dean as an embezzler and a turncoat) ought to have been severely shaken by Watergate. The fact is that respectability and lying often go hand in hand. Moreover, even if it looked as if Dean was not telling the whole truth about the $4,850 he abstracted for his honeymoon from the slush fund of $15,200 he was keeping in his safe, this did not prove that he was lying when he identified Nixon, Haldeman, and Ehrlichman as having participated in the cover-up.

When pressed by Senator Gurney to explain how he had used the money (nearly five thousand dollars for a two-week honeymoon that in the end never came off?), he seemed at a loss for answers that would "add up." My own guess was that he had used a large chunk of that money—which he later paid back—to give his wife a rather large chunk of jewelry and for some reason was embarrassed to admit it. Maureen ("Mo") Dean, who appears in the Caucus Room in a daily change of costume (sometimes color-harmonizing with her husband), looks like a bride who would want fresh jewelry for her honeymoon, like the fresh "lingerie touches" she wears at her throat and wrists.

A Maupassant story with a plot closing like a mousetrap on the ambitious young husband with his frowning mouse-like face.

Tanned the first day and gradually turning sallow, he is not what the public expected. The effeminate Pretty-Boy image he projected in the news magazines is wrong. Horn-rimmed glasses, small face, small neatly set ears, hair growing thin at the crown, he appears more like a history or economics professor at a Middle Western university looking up from a carefully prepared lecture text. The voice, which has grown tired, is low, slightly nasal, Basic American, with notes of his native Ohio still in it. He declines theatrics and the boyish penitent style of his predecessor in the witness chair, Jeb Magruder, and has better grammar on the whole. His manner can be coldly saturnine, like that of a professor rebuffing an over-familiar student. On being asked by Senator Montoya whether he felt "better now," he answered "I am not here as a sinner in a confessional." Above all, he seems determined to present his testimony in a clear, succinct, orderly fashion; any inadvertences that creep in cause him to frown—with an apologetic cough, he goes back to correct himself for a minor slip of the memory or the tongue.

There is no outward sign of the New Conservative in his vocabulary, no trace of far right ideology. He appears free of any ideology, a strictly functional being, and the only index—if it is one—of rightist extremism was the quality, flashing out occasionally in a terse sardonic sentence, of intellectual contempt. The impression, not so much of a truthful person as of someone resolved to tell the truth

about this particular set of events because his intelligence
has warned him to do so, was overpowering during the first
sessions, lasting two days and a half. Then, late Wednesday
afternoon, Senator Inouye began his inquisition, reading
aloud from a memo prepared by Buzhardt, one of the
White House lawyers.

Inouye, a Democrat and one-armed war veteran from
Hawaii, had assumed on his own initiative the role of ad-
versary lawyer and undertaken to confront Dean with the
set of allegations drawn up by the White House. Bold,
frightening allegations designed to rattle Dean's confidence
and shake public confidence in him—an effect that was almost immediately visible in the spectators' section, where
eyes were uneasily searching other eyes for reassurance. If
a poll had been taken at six o'clock on Wednesday, the
jury, though still in Dean's favor, might well have been
split.

The Buzhardt memo was far cleverer than the long cross-
examination we had just heard from Senator Gurney.
Gurney had acted too much like a silky defense attorney
trying to weaken the witness by a series of "damning" questions ("Did you advise the President of the United States
about that?" "No, I did not." "Did you advise the President of the United States about *that?*" "No, I did not"),
the answers to which the senators and the public already
knew. That Dean did not "advise" the President of what
was going on, *i.e.*, keep him "filled in," and why he did not,
had been made abundantly clear in his six-hour opening
statement. The explanation lay in the character of the President, so inaccessible of approach except through the fear-

41

The Mask of State

some "channels" of Haldeman and Ehrlichman, and in Dean's own persuasion that Nixon was fully informed of the cover-up, following it if not actually directing it at every step.

What else was Dean to think after September 15, when he was called in to receive Presidential congratulations on the "job" he had done? On that red-letter day the grand jury, thanks to Dean's activities, had finally indicted seven men (Hunt, McCord, Liddy, and the four Cubans) for the Watergate break-in and left the White House in the clear. You do not rush to tell the Chief Executive the details of a criminal operation of which he has shown you he is cognizant and which he obviously prefers not to have mentioned. Not unless you are a simpleton, which Dean is far from. He had got the hang of a closed system in which crimes are not named by their names—burglary, perjury, pay-offs—but expedited through a process of euphemism. As Ehrlichman said to Dean, when Dean at a late stage tried to talk to him *in so many words* about the hush money being paid to the convicted men: "I always assumed the money was for humanitarian purposes." Or as "Chuck" Colson said the other night on television, when asked about the White House enemies list, a political murder-instrument, "Why, that was just a list we kept of people not to ask to White House functions." Compare the "Final Solution," *toutes proportions gardées*, naturally.

Unlike Senator Gurney's examination, the Buzhardt questions and comments read to the witness in a stern voice by Senator Inouye did not resort to hint or innuendo.

Whereas Gurney had seemed to put the White House in a defensive posture, feebly jabbing at Dean's obvious weak points (the honeymoon money, the TV license), here it was on the offensive, charging in hard. This was the real Nixonian style. Dean had described it himself earlier in his testimony, when he told of the advice Nixon had given him: " 'You've got to fight back.' He made a gesture of striking his fist into his hand. 'You got to keep fighting back.' " So he ought to have been prepared for the brutal attack Inouye was launching on him. Soon a direct accusation came that drew a stunned laugh, almost a gasp, from the audience. "Dean's activity in the cover-up also made him, perhaps unwittingly, the principal author of the political and constitutional crisis that Watergate now epitomizes." The memo had been building up to this awesome moment. Dean was "one of the architects"; he was "perfectly situated to master-mind and carry out a cover-up." Not only the cover-up. Hadn't he been involved in Operation Sand-wedge, an earlier intelligence-gathering project that never got off the ground? Wasn't it he who had introduced Liddy to his "patron," John Mitchell, thereby laying the fatal cornerstone for Watergate? With Mitchell, he had sat in on meetings whose final result was the break-in. It was Dean who had sought to entice the CIA into paying hush money, Dean who two days after the burglary had sent a message to Hunt ordering him to flee the country. It was Dean and Mitchell together who had prepared Magruder for "perjurious testimony," Dean who had said to Colson, "Destroy the memo." To the President, of course, Dean "gave no hint of his own orchestration of perjured testimony." When pressed by Haldeman to produce a written report on Watergate, had he ever produced it? No.

Some of this (and there was much more) was undeniably true and was lifted straight from Dean's own testimony. He *had* been involved with, if not in, Operation Sand-wedge; he *had* introduced Liddy to Mitchell. He had (on Ehrlichman's instructions, he said) talked to General Walters of the CIA to try to get CIA help in "taking care" of their former operatives who had been apprehended in the break-in. On Ehrlichman's order (he said), he had sent the message telling Hunt to get out of the country. He had prepared Magruder to commit perjury before the grand jury. He had never produced the Watergate report. But he had not (he attested) told Colson to destroy a memo; on the contrary, he had taken care to preserve it and had turned a copy of it over to the Committee. Mitchell was not his "patron" or "sponsor" at the White House; that had been Egil Krogh. He had attended meetings where Liddy had presented plans, but at the third and final meeting, when, Magruder said, Watergate was decided on, he had not been present. No one had proposed that he had been aware, even, that it was taking place.

The amalgam of fact removed from context, half-fact, and sheer assertion was topped off by a deft use of his own statement to the Committee that he had not been surprised by news of the break-in when it reached him June 18, on his return from the Philippines. "You were not surprised," suggested Senator Inouye, echoing the memo, "because you were the author of the plan." Now the audience could gasp no more. Rather silently, as the session ended, it filed out of the room.

The outline or "thrust," as these younger bureaucrats like to say, of the White House counter-attack was plain. It had already been faintly visible in the Magruder testimony, which in retrospect seemed to be staking out the pattern. Mitchell and Dean were to be the fall guys. To use White House terminology, reminiscent of gangland, they had been "set up." Still, the *effrontery* of the charge took one's breath away. It was as if a sudden parade of heavy sophisticated weaponry, a sortie of deadly tanks from the White House, had been drawn up before the young witness and his "ally," Nixon's loyal old friend and law partner. Dean, who had thought truth was his weapon, appeared shaken. His answers, in certain areas, became guarded, as though he guessed them to be mined. Did the White House have some dynamite, perhaps in the form of tapes, genuine or doctored, planted in his path that would explode if he did not walk warily?

What Dean did not know (nor did any of us that day) was that the menacing memo prepared by Buzhardt, his own successor as special White House counsel, had not been intended for publication. It had been given to the Committee for "background" use, to direct them to a line of questioning, and Inouye, very courageously, had decided to try to defuse it by reading not just the questions but also the comments aloud in open session. He was exposing the White House hand. On Wednesday afternoon, though, the White House hand, even turned face up for all to see, appeared very powerful. It looked as if Dean were now

45

being made to pay for the leaks he and his friends and the Committee staff had given in advance to the press. Nixon and his men had profited from those leaks and from the week-long Brezhnev recess to construct a model that matched in massive detail—dates, names, places—the model Dean would present, with one salient difference, that he would be in the center of it, revealed as the arch-villain, when the wrappings were torn off. Not only did the memo take account of every significant episode figuring in Dean's testimony but it contrived to cut and tailor each bolt and scrap to make a suit of clothes that fitted Dean and Dean only.

Or put it another way. It was as if Dean in the witness chair were staring at an image of his own account in a distorting mirror, an image recognizable to him point by point but implacably, hallucinatingly different. The situation changed the next day; the optics were brought back to normal by the senators who followed Inouye and in particular by Senator Weicker of Connecticut, a giant Republican who brought the afternoon session to a rousing close by a "fightin' mad" speech. Lowell Weicker revealed to the Committee that he himself was the target of a smear campaign mounted by the White House, with the object, he believed, of obstructing his work in the Committee's investigation. The word was being passed that contributions to his 1970 campaign for the Senate had been illegally or improperly handled. Recently, "Chuck" Colson had tried to plant the Weicker story on a reporter from a Washington newspaper—Colson being the White House specialist in this field: he had been peddling the Kennedy cable crudely fabricated by Howard Hunt (implicating Kennedy in Diem's assassination) to *Life* magazine.

Weicker's dander was up. That morning he had lodged a complaint with the Special Prosecutor, Archibald Cox, to demonstrate that he meant business: the penalty for obstructing the work of a Congressional committee—a federal crime—is five thousand dollars or five years in jail or both. Rising in his seat, as if bodily lifted by civic indignation, the junior Senator from Connecticut, a rich man in his own right (Squibb, Bigelow Sanford), shouted a warning to the White House: "There are going to be no more threats, no intimidation, no innuendo, no working through the press to go ahead and destroy the credibility of individuals. If the executive branch of the government wants to meet the standards that the American people set for it in their mind, then the time has come to stop. . . ." Wild clapping from the public, a rush, as the session closed, to thank the Senator, felicitate him. With his great bulk and the admirers surrounding him, he looked like the newly crowned champion in some spectacular sporting event.

Weicker was making no bones of his willingness to identify his own case with Dean's. He removed his senatorial purple to present himself as a fellow smear target. And, though he did not state it explicitly, he was handing the Committee evidence of an ongoing effort at cover-up that put the accusations against Dean in a funny light. Dean, after all, could hardly be the "principal author" of what was happening to Weicker. There must be someone else, behind the scenes.

What was finally reflected in a shadowy corner of the

distorting mirror that had been held up to Dean for his terrified inspection was—again—the character of Nixon. All along, as a matter of fact, the general sense that Dean was telling the truth had been strengthened by the touches of awful veracity in his character study of the President and of the paranoid atmosphere surrounding him. Nobody could make those things up. The man with the sign in Lafayette Park, opposite the White House; the demonstrator who had "charged" the car during the inaugural parade, *i.e.,* who had tried to get through the crowd to make his protest and who became the object of a man hunt in which Petersen, Silbert (both high up in Justice), the Secret Service, and Haldeman had been made to join (to Nixon's fury, the police had caught the demonstrator, found he had no weapon, and let him go); the promise, or ogre's threat, to "make some dramatic changes in all the agencies" after the election; the book Dean found him reading one day— *The Twelve Mistakes of Kennedy.*

Add Dean's belief that Nixon did not understand the implications of the course of action he was taking, shown, for instance, in the strange reply he gave Dean, who, by that time very fearful of the uncovering of the cover-up, tried to tell him in plain words, such as "perjury," "obstruction of justice," what they were all doing. "After I finished I realized that I had not really made the President understand because after he asked a few questions he suggested that it would be an excellent idea if I gave some sort of briefing to the Cabinet and that he was very impressed with my knowledge of the circumstances." This claustral, obsessive personality was served by familiars suited to the ambience. Add Ehrlichman's taste (resembling a sexual perversion) for leftist demonstrations: "Like a Dalmatian dog at a fire. He can't stay away from them." And Haldeman and Ehrlichman, thinking themselves unobserved, laughing in the White House corridor as they leave the Oval Office; inside, the President is waiting with a choice of two letters of resignation in his desk drawer for Dean to sign, and they know they have set Dean up like a lone pin in a bowling alley.

Listening to the soft-voiced Inouye level point-blank the charges packed into the White House memo, remembering the peculiar slant or tilt of Magruder's seemingly ingenuous testimony, one could get the eerie feeling that Dean had been "set up" from the beginning, while he was flying back from the Philippines on the eighteenth of June still oblivious of Watergate. They must have long ago taken Dean's measure: his courier-like eagerness to show his usefulness, his pride in himself as the White House "fire-fighter," his undoubted ability, power of swift thinking, analysis, organization, and the crucial fact that he "belonged" to Mitchell, their rival, who might also have to be "set up" or "smoked out" (another White House phrase) if need be. That is, if anybody got caught. Whoever planned Watergate must have reckoned with the possibility of a slip-up. In that case, a fixer would be wanted, and a fixer on whom the blame could be pinned if the fix did not stick. Dean is clever but does not appear to be particularly cunning, and Haldeman and Ehrlichman may always have been a stage ahead of him in their calculations. While he was busy exercising his zeal to be useful, they may have foreseen a handy use for him and his zeal—should scape-goat time arrive—that went beyond his own modest conception of service. And if nobody got caught at the Watergate, the young special counsel (who had that TV license against him) might win his stripes on some other suicide mission.

Late in the game, as Dean related in a characteristically vivid bit of testimony, Haldeman told him that "if the cover-up was to proceed, we would have to draw the wagons in a circle around the White House and the White House would protect only itself." The wagons are now drawn up around the stockade. Inside are Nixon, General Haig, and the spirits of Haldeman and Ehrlichman; Colson is up in a tree picking off the enemy; Magruder is trying to infiltrate back. Dean has been smoked out, Mitchell has been smoked out, but that feral old dog (whom Dean tried to spare in his testimony) may stay faithful, circling around the perimeter, despite the savage mistreatment given him in the last few days, and trying to scare away the senators with his bark.

A
Steady
Dosage
of
Lies

July 15, 1973

Even before Thursday evening, when Nixon went into
Bethesda Naval Hospital, the estimate here was that he
could not weather Watergate. Now, naturally, that feeling is
stronger. Yet it comes at a time when the Senate hearings
are faltering. The Caucus Room all week has had a new
atmosphere, of disaffection, boredom, almost disgust. The
performances of the Ervin panel senators, the quality of
their staff work are reviewed by journalists with mounting
impatience. The press tables stand partly empty, and the
front-row VIP seats are denuded a good deal of the day.
At one of the long, semi-deserted press tables Wednesday
afternoon a small child sat drawing airplanes and what
looked like big bombs in red crayon on a sheet of yellow
paper, which he then folded into a glider, unfortunately
aimless. Photostats of the Mitchell logs lie around collecting dust; many who got them as a hand-out did not bother
to take them home.

The credit or responsibility for this devastation belongs
to John Mitchell, whose sodden-voiced testimony occupied
most of three days that came to resemble eternity in its
hellish aspect. Outside, early in the week, an air-pollution
alert had been sounded, as if in sympathy: people with eye
or respiratory problems were warned to make no exertion
and/or to stay indoors; according to rumor, a radio broad-

cast had told the population to refrain from drinking tea
and coffee, though not, apparently, alcohol. There can be
no greater boredom, I think, than that engendered by a
steady dosage of lies. As Mitchell testified, the occasional
laughter of the first day that met his toneless disavowals,
the hiss that susurrated once through the room were re-
placed by an almost total sound vacuum, which in some
dulled helpless way matched the calculated void of his
contribution.

It was true that the performances of the senators—with
one exception—and of counsel were poor, but they had had
him Monday in executive session and thus got a preview of
the public charade. That they had come out of that wilted
and blanched was understandable, for there was nothing
human or responsive in the element they had been im-
mersed in. Stone-walling, Senator Weicker, the only brave
man of the week, called it, borrowing the phrase, in fact,
from the sinister White House lexicon. Trying to get a direct answer from John Mitchell *was* like beating your head
against a stone wall. Faced with two diametrically opposed
statements given under oath by himself, he blandly declined
to see any contradiction. Weicker, angry: "Is this your defi-
nition, by the way, this kind of testimony, of, what is the
expression, of 'stone-walling it'?" Mitchell, insolent: "I
don't know that term. Is that a Yankee term from Connecticut?" Connecticut is Senator Weicker's home state.

The fear of another perjury indictment—he has been
charged already in New York in the Vesco matter—might
seem to be a rational explanation for his obtuseness to any
trace of contradiction when shown a pair of his own state-

ments one of which cannot be true. Yet to play blind to a contradiction does not prevent others from perceiving it. Moreover, the Senate panel, far from being out to "get" Mitchell, appeared bent merely on getting some truth from him, using those discrepancies, finally, as a press to squeeze it out. But it was a case of trying to get blood from a turnip, and indeed there was something turnipy about Mitchell, the off-white (or tattletale gray) face with occasional mottlings of purplish pink, the watery, squelchy voice, the smooth bald pate.

He was educated, at Fordham University and Fordham Law School, by the Jesuits, though he is a Protestant, and vocally and visually he has that root-cellar quality of the Jesuitic world, at least as I knew it in my Catholic childhood—the small lifeless eyes, like those of a wintering potato, the voice sprouting insinuations. He is supposed to have been an athlete, a hockey player and golfer, but you would never guess it to look at his sedentary outline, sloping-headed, slope-shouldered, slope-nosed, without tone or elasticity. The mind is not supple, merely practiced in weary equivocation.

When I started listening to Mitchell, I did the normal thing—tried to ask myself what truth there might be in the story he was telling. For instance, about the Liddy plan. All accounts agreed that it had been presented to him three times, on a descending scale of grandiosity (from kidnapping, prostitutes, mugging, a yacht, to mere breaking-and-entry and bugging), the first two in his Attorney General's office at the Justice Department, the last on March 30 at Key Biscayne. All accounts agreed that he had twice rejected it. Magruder said that the third time he had given a reluctant consent. Dean, who had not been present at Key Biscayne, was unable to testify on the point. Mitchell himself denied that he had ever given his approval. On the contrary. " 'We don't need this. Out. Let's not discuss it any further.' " According to him, he assumed the project had been killed then and there. When he heard of the Watergate break-in, it did "cross his mind" that this was the old Liddy plan, finally put into operation, but he dismissed the thought because "the players were different"—McCord and some Cubans. Not, at that time, Liddy, whose involvement only came to light some days later.

Plausible, so far, though maybe not likely. Mitchell's word against Magruder's. The only backing for Magruder's story came from McCord, who said Liddy had told him that Mitchell had given his approval, and from another witness, Reisner, who said that the Gemstone material—the code name for Watergate—had been put by Magruder in a file marked "Mitchell." But perhaps that could be explained.

Still another witness, Fred LaRue, whom Mitchell expects to back him up since he was present at the third meeting, will take a middle position, if the information Senator Weicker, on Wednesday morning, claimed to have is right. He will say that Mitchell neither rejected nor approved but deferred decision on the plan. For LaRue we shall have to wait.

Meanwhile, in Mitchell's favor was the fact that Magruder, once a Haldeman favorite, had seemed, at least to me, a questionable witness bent on playing the White House loyalist game of fingering Mitchell and Dean. And if it appeared unlikely that the quite junior Magruder could have okayed Watergate on his own, in defiance of Mitchell's express order to drop it, it might be that Magruder had been acting on instructions from some higher authority. "In hindsight," Mitchell now said (a favorite barbarism with him; *cf. OED:* "1. The backsight of a rifle. 1851. Mayne Reid *Scalp Hunt.* xxi, When you squint through her hindsights"), he thought there *had* been pressures on Magruder. When asked by the Majority Counsel if these pressures could have come "from above," Mitchell grew wary. They could have come from "collateral areas"—not necessarily from above. He declined to "speculate," but "collateral areas" meant Colson, as the initiate immediately understood.

Up to now, the story held up—just barely. But from that point on, all questions glanced off him. He denied having had the faintest awareness of any activity leading up to the break-in. Hadn't he authorized a "substantial sum" to be paid to Liddy? No, that was Magruder. But Sloan said differently, Maurice Stans said differently.

Dash: Let me just read to you, Mr. Mitchell, Mr. Stans's testimony: "I said, do you mean, John, that if Magruder tells Sloan to pay these amounts or any amounts to Gordon Liddy, that he should? And he said, 'That is right.'"
Mitchell: Well, I would respectfully disagree with Mr. Stans.

No attempt was made to lend some minimal plausibility to his denials, to his repeated "I don't recall" concerning crucial incidents. On a single occasion: "Must be a confusion of persons." The weariness and boredom of his voice suggested that all this was ridiculous, preposterous, but also that he could not take the trouble to work up a lie that somebody might conceivably believe. He seemed rancorously determined to insult the intelligence of the Committee, the press, the TV audience—everybody, the world at large. His testimony was held together not in the usual way, in terms of general likelihood and known facts outside itself, but by an inner wooden logic based on speaking *for the record*. When examined, it would contain nothing tending toward an admission. In other words pointing toward truth or reality.

Hence the interrogation grew so intolerably boring. There was none of that element of danger that can make clever lying, up to a point, exciting to the liar and to those who watch and listen, since clever lying always has large amounts of truth mixed into it, which tend to both support the fabrication and imperil it: even little bits of truth may undo you by hanging together in an unforeseen way.

With the ex-Attorney General, one did not feel oneself in the presence of even half- or quarter-truths, which one might start trying to piece together with other information to get a reasonable whole. To do that, one has to disregard every statement and non-statement about Watergate made by Mitchell under oath to the Senate Committee. Except for the initial assertion: that he did *not* approve the third presentation of the Liddy plan at Key Biscayne. Accepting that provisionally as true, how can we interpret what followed? If he postponed decision (as LaRue may presently testify), Liddy and his sponsors while he vacillated might have elected to bypass him. Suppose Mitchell soon sensed, when consulted about those large sums for Liddy, that someone else had given approval over his head, someone, singular or plural, who had been pushing it all along, someone who had sold the notion to the President (or hadn't, whichever seems more likely). When the project came up the third time, over his double veto, Mitchell must already have known, and not by hindsight, that powerful forces were sanctioning it. So what did he decide to do? Play along and play possum. If the scheme succeeded, he was in the clear, having taken no further steps to block it. If it failed, he was in the clear, since his opposition was, he thought, on the record. If it succeeded, the team as a whole gained; if it failed, his enemies on the team would be discredited. Nothing would be lost by keeping a "low profile."

He may not have rated the risks of the operation high enough and have thought more in terms of financial gamble, seeing the plan as a probable waste of campaign funds, than in terms of the burglars actually getting caught on the premises and with Committee to Re-elect money and a White House telephone number on them. Hitherto, in the various Plumbers' and dirty tricks forays, nobody had been caught, and one may assume (if one wants) that Mitchell of course knew about them, despite his denials to the Senate panel. Anyway, he probably did not foresee that the burglars would let themselves be caught flat-footed, thus depriving the CRP of precious "deniability," which it still would have had if they could have got away, leaving only the "bugs" and signs of forcible entry behind them.

The sequel can be outlined almost any way you like.

After the break-in, Mitchell told Nixon what he knew. Or he did not tell him. Either because he knew Nixon knew already or because he was not sure whether Nixon knew or not and wanted to leave him that same deniability. It may be a literal fact that Nixon never asked him, although many people find that unbelievable. It *is* unbelievable if you assume Nixon knew nothing, but if you take the opposite assumption, there is no problem. The twin assertions made by Mitchell—that Nixon did not know and never asked—would be believable only on one condition: Nixon is a psychopath who adhered throughout Watergate to his own sick certainty that everything disseminated by the media is false and hence of no interest, except as further evidence of a design to persecute him.

That, even so, his entourage did not seek to alert him appears strange, unless fear was the reason. Mitchell testified that he did not tell the President the horrors that had been going on for fear that he would "lower the boom," meaning fire everybody concerned and thus create a noisome scandal. Yet, as Senator Inouye pointed out, if and when the President at last learned something approaching the truth, no boom was lowered: only Dean, who had been warning him, like the king's messenger, about the spreading "cancer," got the axe. So if there really was general apprehension about what Nixon would do were the facts to reach him, it was unlikely to have stemmed from dread of a rational response, such as a strenuous housecleaning. Indeed, as was shown in Dean's testimony (". . . he suggested that it would be an excellent idea if I gave a briefing to the Cabinet") and again, Friday, in that of the fatherly media expert Richard Moore, Nixon's actual responses to Watergate disclosures were alarming in their dreamy inertia. Moore advised him forcefully on April 20 to get outside counsel. "And what did the President do?" "He went to Key Biscayne."

Mitchell's reason, as given by him, for shielding Nixon from the realities was not nervousness about Watergate, which he dismissed as insignificant. It was the knowledge he had got from Liddy, via LaRue and Mardian, of the "White House horror stories." This, it transpired, was another of Mitchell's private code names for Colson, the promoter of Hunt and Liddy. The horrors comprised the sequestering of Dita Beard in a hide-away hospital, with Hunt in a red wig by her bedside, the raid on the office of Ellsberg's psychiatrist, the forging of the Diem cables, the project for fire-bombing the Brookings Institution, "extra-curricular wiretapping," the private-eye job at Chappaquiddick. He did not name any other horrors, preferring cryptic innuendoes to what he called "specifics."

He did not care for the words "cover-up" and "perjury." "What is being referred to here as the cover-up," he would repeat, and for lying under oath, "We were not volunteering information." Though sensitive to the injury words did, he was fond of "the Democrat National Committee," "the Democrat party"—shades of the late Senator Joe McCarthy, who never said "Democratic," seeming to believe that clipping a syllable from the regular name was powerful black magic, like clipping bits of your enemy's toenails to snip his vital forces. "Democrat," in Joe McCarthy's and Mitchell's evil parlance (and also, by the way, in Senator

Gurney's), seemed to do double duty as a cipher for leftish, Commie-tainted.

Mitchell brought evil into the Caucus Room, and this was not unconnected with the boredom he was able to generate—many thought deliberately—turning spectators who had been constituting a sort of town meeting into a restless, anomic, a-political crowd. After several days of him, nobody cared whether Nixon knew or not, whether Haldeman and Ehrlichman planned the cover-up, or even whether Mitchell's own toneless and non-responsive testimony was being dictated by the earlier threats from the White House implicit in the show of force of the Buzhardt memo.

Still, there was a mystery about that memo. Hardly had it become public, thanks to Senator Inouye's reading it aloud in open session, than it was disavowed by the Western White House. The President, his aides said, had been briefed on its contents but he was not its author. In any case, it was only Buzhardt's own "version" or "hypothesis." A few days later Buzhardt gave an interview to the Washington *Post*; Nixon, he insisted, was as confused as anybody else about who had been responsible for Watergate. In fact he (Buzhardt) admitted to being confused himself. Then why had he drawn up the memo for the Committee's private guidance in questioning Dean or had he merely signed it and sent it over to the Committee? If so, who wrote it? "Anon."? Clearly it was a trial balloon of some sort which was allowed to float off on its own into the stratosphere once its purpose had been served.

The purpose, one has to guess, was to send a warning signal to Mitchell, sequestered in his New York apartment and drinking heavily. Even had the full memo never been read aloud, Mitchell would have got its drift from the line of questioning it prompted. Since the Fourth of July recess was coming, he would have had ample time to think it over and send a return signal before his rendezvous with the Committee in public session on Monday, July 8. He was being warned, in unmistakable terms, against talking to the panel. If he was so foolish as to do so, the White House, he could suspect, had evidence at hand to make good its threat, evidence, for example, of his signature or initials on some of the Gemstone material. All that material was supposed to have been burned or shredded, but how could Mitchell be sure that Haldeman, looking toward the future, had not put aside some pieces of paper sufficient to dispose of his old enemy if transmitted to the grand jury?

Senator Inouye, by making the memo public, had perhaps speeded up the exchange of signals between blackmailers and blackmailee. When the Western White House issued its disclaimer, it may already have got a message from Mitchell conceding his surrender. In that case, Inouye's initiative would have sadly misfired; his intention, one assumes, had been to encourage Mitchell to speak out by giving him documentary proof of Nixon's ruthlessness and perfidy toward an old friend and counselor. Maybe Mitchell did not require any further proof of that. Anyhow, however it happened, Mitchell gave in. If for some weeks, at his wife's urging, he had considered speaking out, he had changed his mind by the time he walked into the hearing-room, stolid and heavy-faced. He had agreed to play ball, and the very unresponsiveness of his testimony, his dourness and lethargy were indications, possibly, even signals of his resentment of the duress he was under. No witness ever made it clearer that he was *not talking*. If he truly had not approved the Liddy plan but only gone along with it grudgingly when he recognized that someone else had approved it, he might have won credence and also some sympathy from the senators by vouchsafing the facts as he knew them and disclosing his real part, small or large, in the transactions. A full description of the pressures he had been subject to leading up to June 17 and from June 18 onward, right up to the present moment, could have won him a kind of acquittal. Instead he sat before them stonily, the very picture of a man who had sold his silence.

Curiosity revived when Richard Moore took the witness chair. Fifty-nine years old, pictured by himself as a "source of white-haired advice and experience" for the President (born a year earlier than he), a prominent Son of St. Patrick and former head of the Los Angeles Chamber of Commerce, this White House Nestor restored the atmosphere to something resembling normal, even though he appeared to be in his dotage and had practically nothing to contribute—his testimony, which was supposed to controvert Dean's, in fact corroborated it on almost every point. The forgetful old Republican may have seemed to be foolish, prosy, rather vain, but he also seemed to believe that he was telling the truth or something close to it. At least until Friday, when Senator Weicker caught him in an obvious prevarication on one of the Watergate subsidiary matters and he too began to stone-wall, though with more agitation than Mitchell had shown. His main fault, though, was a sort of commerce-laved innocence. He had thought (and probably still does) that the Watergate cancer could be cured by salesmanship: "Mr. President, why don't we get the story out ourselves?"

There was a long moment, though, on Wednesday when Mitchell's answers awakened sparks of interest. Senator Baker was interrogating, and the area he was covering, that of judgment and opinion, no doubt seemed safe to the witness. He could afford candor; nobody will slap a perjury indictment on you or treat you as a squealer if you stick to ideas. Senator Baker: "What is your perception of the institution of the Presidency?" Mitchell allowed that that would take a long time to answer, but then answers started popping out of him like sulphurous firecrackers. His perception of the institution was that he was unable to contemplate anybody but Richard Nixon in it, as though the presidency had become unique with Nixon's incumbency, different from anything previous and requiring self-succession. He had already stated that, for him, the re-election of this particular President was paramount and justified the cover-up.

He now went on to say, with a brief verbal genuflection (for once showing an emotion; was it the memory of tender worship or just veneration?), that the President could not deal "with all the mundane problems that go on from day to day." He himself had spared him knowledge of the "horror stories" and incidentally Watergate (how a horror story could be mundane was not clear) to relieve him of the need to decide what to do about them. "I had to keep his

65

options open." A decision, if taken, "would have impeded his potential for re-election." "I was not about to countenance anything that would hinder that re-election."

All this was said in tones of self-evidence: he was setting out propositions so axiomatic that they needed no demonstration. Nor did he seem to be aware of the enormity of what he was enunciating—a doctrine of a higher law transcending the Constitution, incarnate in the figure of our old friend Tricky Dick. He made not the slightest allusion to *policies* that might call for continuance but merely insisted on the person of Nixon (whom he also referred to as "the individual"), whose sole function seemed to be getting re-elected, like a perpetual-motion machine. This then, pulling at its pipe, was a sample of a proto-fascist mentality or its deposed Grand Vizier. We had half expected some revelation of the kind from the "Germans" Haldeman and Ehrlichman but hardly from an old-style, coarse, crony-type law-and-order politician and backroom mouthpiece.

The relations of the Nixon band among each other, shadowing forth the parallel structures of totalitarian organizations (see Hannah Arendt's *The Origins of Totalitarianism*), received—and not for the first time in these hearings —a little illumination from the Mitchell testimony, and this ray of light too was cast almost inadvertently, as if casually, when Mitchell "happened" to mention a detail of an interview with Ehrlichman that took place this last mid-April in Ehrlichman's office. By this time Mitchell was out of the power arena, his usefulness having ended when the lid started blowing off the cover-up; at earlier meetings the two had sat at a coffee table. Now they sat near the desk as

Ehrlichman questioned him about the extent of his Watergate involvement. The shift in the seating arrangements, duly noted by Mitchell, was not just emblematic; he instantly surmised, as if it were the most natural thing in the world, that there was a listening-device hidden somewhere in the region of the desk.

A
Bomb
in the
White House

July 22, 1973

When he left the White House, four months ago, they were becoming a storage problem, the witness said. Never, to his knowledge, transcribed, simply accumulating in various closets and cupboards in the Executive Office Building basement, the tapes, guarded night and day by Secret Service men, had been made (Butterfield was sure) just to "record things for posterity." In his time, their existence and that of their parent devices in the Oval Office, the Executive Office Building office, and the Cabinet Room were known only to the President, Haldeman, Butterfield's superior Lawrence Higby, Butterfield himself, and eventually, because it could not be avoided, Butterfield's secretary. And of course the Technical Security Division of the Secret Service, who had installed the system and who checked the working tapes and devices at least daily. Ehrlichman did not know about them. Haldeman had the authority to enter the room where the tapes were, although Butterfield thought it was unlikely that he would have used it. Nobody else except, presumably, some trusted maintenance men.

There were also recording devices on the telephones in the Oval Office and the Lincoln sitting-room in the White House, on the telephones in the Executive Office Building office and at Camp David. The listening-equipment in the Cabinet Room could be turned on and off manually; the remainder of the system functioned automatically, receiv-

ing commands from "locator lights" to stand ready to record whenever the President entered either of his offices.
These President-sensors (horribly evocative of the people-
sensors used in Vietnam to detect hidden Viet Cong), light-
ing up at the Nixonian footfall, could not be switched off,
and in Butterfield's time no order had ever been given to
disconnect the recording system temporarily. The tapes
themselves were "voice-actuated" and sensitive to the bar-
est whisper.

That history was being preserved underground and with
such extreme vigilance, like an atomic secret, hit the Senate
Caucus Room with utter unexpectedness. "We've got a
bombshell for you," Majority Counsel Sam Dash leaned
over to tell his wife (who sits in the VIP row just behind
me) as the Monday afternoon session was about to start.
Explosive material, dynamite, enough to blow the case sky-
high—that was the immediate reaction to the news. And the
immediate assumption was that Nixon would be the victim,
hoist by his own petard: the tapes would confirm Dean.
Anxiety therefore was felt, at least in our corner of the
press section, about the tapes' safety, and we sent a message
of concern up to the Minority Counsel—shouldn't the FBI
be keeping an eye on them too? The moral shock of learning that Nixon had been bugging himself and anybody who
approached his offices since 1971 lost some of its impact in
the general joyful feeling that the case was going to be resolved. It is hard to be shocked and jubilate at the same
time. You had to choose, and the senators, on the whole,
conscious of their position as moral guardians, preferred

shock. But many of their aides and junior counsel were grinning.

The case would resolve, once and for all, the same way it had started, by an inadvertence of technology. We would no longer have to weigh such "subjective" factors as credibility in making up our minds; no need for cross-examination, no need, in fact, to hear any more long-winded witnesses and probe, with Senator Baker, into their motivations. "Sophisticated" technology had come to the country's rescue with those marvelous tapes. If we had only known about them before. What a lot of mental man-hours we would have saved. Having been "sparked" by electronic surveillance, Watergate would terminate, appropriately, by the same means. "Krapp's last tapes," my husband cabled. And this time no bungling. Butterfield reassured Senator Montoya: he felt there was no possibility that any tapes could be missing or destroyed—the President was "very conscious of our having a good system for collecting the things which transpired with regard to the affairs of state."

This mood of exhilaration, of course, did not last. Already that Monday afternoon disquiet began to be felt, no longer just about the safety of the tapes from pilferage but about whether they could be doctored. According to specialists, seized upon in corridors, they could. It was pretty difficult to add anything, but cuts could be made, the tape spliced together, and a fresh tape made from it. On the new tape, there would be no trace of the surgery. By Wednesday, these worries, attributed to unidentified senators, had reached the press. The only question (not raised in the press) was: would Nixon dare? He could not do it him-self (hard to picture him, at night, in pajamas and dressing-gown, slipping downstairs, past Technical Security out to the Executive Office Building, and anyway he was in the hospital), and among his present aides, who was left to help him? Laird? General Haig? The conclusion was: no-body. Unless in the Secret Service, among the guards, there was a Tony Ulasewicz.

As the days passed with no answer from the White House to Senator Ervin's request for the tapes, the bombshell began to feel more and more like an infernal machine tick-ing away in an Executive Office Building cellar cupboard. Did Nixon's holding on to the tapes mean that he knew they confirmed Dean? Or was he saving them, as a last-minute Nixonian surprise to spring on the Committee? A nasty sur-prise like that ("TAPES EXONERATE NIXON") might well be in the cards. To support this nervous hypothesis there came a further question: why in the world was he making the tapes in the first place?

Surely not for the Nixon Library, as Butterfield was con-vinced. If that were the purpose, there would be no reason for the cosmic secrecy. And if not for the Nixon Library, then simply for the sake of total control of his environ-ment? In that case he must have been exercising total con-trol over himself all day long, so that any incriminating voice print left on the tapes would be the other fellow's, not Nixon's. And yet Butterfield said that the President seemed to be uninhibited by the listening-devices. "Really oblivi-ous," he marveled. But a man like Nixon was incapable of *forgetting* that his every word was being recorded. That lack of trepidation was ominous, however you looked at it.

Still another doubt fastened on Butterfield himself. As the excited Committee staff had told the story on Monday, they had learned about the tapes by accident, almost miraculously, because the deputy minority counsel who was interviewing him routinely, as a former member of Haldeman's staff, happened to ask the right question. And Butterfield had answered, on the mistaken assumption that his former superior, Higby, would have already revealed the tapes' existence in *his* interview. In other words, if Higby had told the truth, it would be stupid for Butterfield to deny it. The Committee had been much too grateful to Butterfield during his appearance to question the "loyalist" ethics underlying that proposition—had he made the opposite assumption, would he have lied to his interrogator?

Now, however, after-thoughts arose touching the witness's character and the *luckiness* of the discovery. True, an accidental revelation coming at a crucial juncture, when the hearings were slowing down, could be just that, a stroke of luck, and there was something very fitting in the thought: so much of the Watergate story, starting with the passing of the night watchman, Frank Wills, on his rounds, and the chance presence of a prowl car in the neighborhood, has hung on accidents, as though offended reality were bent on showing its power—unpredictability—to the Nixon controllers and managers. But in the atmosphere of growing uneasiness generated by those infernal machines biding their time in that basement, some people were beginning to ask whether Butterfield might not be a plant, poisoned bait set before the Committee to prepare for the release of the tapes. After all, he had been recruited by Haldeman and was an old Haldeman chum. Some suspicion, quite unjustly, even attached to the fact that it was minority, *i.e.*, Republican, counsel that stumbled on the information.

Then, Thursday afternoon, came the hoax, the telephone call to Senator Ervin from somebody posing as Secretary of the Treasury Shultz (the Secret Service is under the Treasury) to announce that the President had decided to make available to the Committee tapes of conversations "he may have had with witnesses before the Committee." If there had been any doubt about the authenticity of the message, that "may have had" settled it; it was as good as a Nixon autograph on a football. But there was no doubt (as Senator Ervin said later, "I guess I believed it because I thought it was what the President *ought* to do"), and the misgivings that followed the announcement by Ervin were only the same four-day-old misgivings: if Nixon was releasing the tapes, it was because they could not hurt him.

Either they had been hastily doctored between Monday and Thursday or they had been fixed in advance, when Haldeman still had access—there had been a whole month to do it in, once Dean's going to the prosecutors early in April had sounded an alarm. Or else Dean was lying, and the vast consensus that thought he was telling the truth was wrong. Perhaps this alternative was the hardest to look in the eye, not because of Nixon hatred but because one does not want to have been wrong in such a crucial judgment. To have been wrong threatened one's sense of reality, the very sense one had been defending against the sellers of the

President, a *common* sense that had seemed to be embodied in the portly figure of Senator Ervin, the "country lawyer," with his North Carolina stories and his store of quotations from Shakespeare and the Bible, kept in a sort of preserve jar and shared out to the hungry population.

Then, within fifteen minutes, the hoax was exposed. A follow-up call from Dash to White House counsel produced an instant denial. There was whispered conferring at the senatorial table, and Senator Ervin hurriedly left the Caucus Room, followed by a flying wedge of the press corps, to step into a public phone booth and ring Secretary Shultz. He came back, red-faced and spluttering (this was perhaps his most sympathetic moment in the hearings up to now), to confess that he had been had, and the public settled down again to listen to the afternoon's witness—Mardian, a former assistant attorney general, almost indistinguishable from the morning's witness, LaRue, both bald, sharp-nosed, tanned clerkly types wearing glinting metal-rimmed glasses and scarcely differing in the main outlines of their testimony. Though each contradicted the other on some rather minor matters, the effect of the contradictions was to cancel out the areas of disagreement, rendering them as null as the witnesses themselves.

Did Mitchell, when told about the Gemstone file still in the CREEP offices, suggest that Jeb Magruder "have a fire"? LaRue said yes; Mardian said no, not in his hearing, though he had been present at the meeting referred to. What about the meeting when Magruder "indicated" that he was going to commit perjury—was Mardian present? LaRue said yes; Mardian said no. Mardian denied LaRue's assertion that he had arranged an interview with Liddy on June 20, three days after the break-in, but agreed that he had been there. Some of Mardian's denials were self-protective: having been an assistant attorney general before he went to CREEP, he knew that any admission of complicity in the Watergate cover-up, given his law-enforcement background, would have made him particularly liable to indictment. But his own complicity or lack of it was less interesting to the Committee than what he had to tell about Mitchell, his former chief. Both Mardian and LaRue had belonged to the hard core of gray Mitchell men; LaRue, however, who had pleaded guilty to obstruction of justice and was co-operating with the government in the hope of staying out of jail, showed a franker willingness to compromise Mitchell. Mardian, for example, when asked whether Mitchell on June 18 had "confirmed" to him having approved a dirty-tricks and black-advance budget (*i.e.*, Watergate) made a hedging reply: "It is my best recollection that I think the subject was discussed and he didn't deny it. And again it may have come up when Mr. Mitchell wasn't in the room. I want to be fair on that point." On the other hand, testifying about a slightly later meeting (June 23 or 24), he said that Mitchell had silently "acquiesced" in Magruder's statement that a $250,000 budget for Liddy had been authorized by him. LaRue went further, not only in testifying about the proposed "fire"—he said that Mitchell, consulted this past March, advised him to go ahead and "make the delivery" of $75,000 worth of hush money. Yet on the vital question of the Key Biscayne meeting, LaRue's long-awaited testimony, if anything, slightly favored Mitchell. Contrary to Magruder's allegation, Mitchell had *not* approved the plan for electronic surveillance presented to him that day: he had said "something to the effect that 'Well, this is not something that will have to be decided at this meeting.' " Yet LaRue could not agree that this had constituted a rejection, which would have brought his testimony close to confirming Mitchell's.

This was a pity; *three* conflicting versions were one too many. If any substantial agreement could be reached on Mitchell's role in the planning and initiating of Watergate, we would be well on the track of the truth. The elimination of Mitchell as the main suspect, the brain that authorized the plan if it had not actually fathered it, would clear the ground and allow other possibilities to emerge into the light. That he played an active part in the cover-up is no longer subject to doubt. The colorlessness of the Tweedle-dum-Tweedledee testimony of Mardian and LaRue, their inclination to cancel each other out as in a game of tick-tacktoe tended to obscure the fact that they were nevertheless almost naively informative about the cover-up operation and the unquestioning readiness of the Mitchell circle, including themselves, to take part in it.

Here is a nice snatch of Friday morning's testimony:

Senator Talmadge: Did you ask Mr. LaRue if he had known about the break-in ahead of time?
Mardian: I cannot recall any specific time I said, Fred, did you know about it ahead of time, until after these hearings started. He called me and told me that he was going to the U.S. Attorney's office and I asked him on that occasion, Fred, did you know about it ahead of time? And he said, yes. Pardon me. The question I

asked him was not specifically about the break-in itself. Did he know about the activities? And he said, yes.

Q. Did you ask him if John knew?

A. My next question, as I recall it, at that time was did John know about it ahead of time? He said, yes.

Q. And you were referring to John Mitchell?

A. Yes. I then said what does John say? He says John says no. Now, subsequently, after my appearance before, I believe, the grand jury, I talked to Fred. He called me and asked me about what had transpired with reference to him. I related what I just told you, and Fred said, My God, you did not say that, did you? And I said yes. And he said, Bob, I do not think I said that.

But now, on Friday morning, few are taking an interest in Mardian. A leak from the White House has just told us that the President on Monday will refuse to turn over the tapes. That is the news of the day, and the public is already looking ahead to next week and the next chapter. A confrontation can be expected, which will have its own sporting excitement. But even if Nixon in the end does turn over the tapes, or is forced to, we shall have lost the happy illusion that they will settle anything. Only if they back up Dean will most people trust them, I think. First of all because they will confirm what was already believed, though maybe with some unexpected variations; second, because it is difficult to see how Dean could have forged them by dubbing in the President's voice, even if this were technically possible and even if, during his tenure, he knew of the listening-system, which, according to Butterfield, he could not have. Should they fail to back up Dean, the suspicion will remain that they have been doctored. This may seem unjust to Nixon, but it is the price he pays for privily recording his associates and relying, if he does, on the tapes to crush them.

The trouble with a tape is that, unlike a witness, you cannot cross-examine it. If it has been cut, it will not say so. Unlike a witness, it can only repeat what is on it and carries no trace of its history in its countenance and demeanor. The alleged watchfulness of the guardians is no guarantee, since guardians are corruptible and also doze on the job or step out for a cup of coffee.

Should the tapes back up Dean, it will go hard on Nixon, but in that case it is unlikely that we shall see or hear them. Perhaps we shall be told that some have been damaged by atmospheric conditions in the room where they were kept, though most people say that is too crude—Nixon would not dare. But he has dared a great deal, before now, and what is to prevent Ziegler's saying that owing to a leak in the cellar the tapes have become "inoperative"? At this moment, Nixon may have only boldness on his side. He is on the run, and there are no portals open for him to dart into. The doctrine of executive privilege will not give him asylum if Special Prosecutor Archie Cox demands the tapes (which may well be the next step), since Cox is part of the Executive. Assuming he refuses and Cox then resigns, Nixon's guilt will be all but proclaimed. If he believed in his own innocence, it would seem, and in the perfection of his recording and storage system, he would produce the tapes, even though he despaired of their persuasive power over a skeptical nation.

The attitude of the Committee during Thursday's hoax is interesting in this respect. The elation of Senator Ervin as he announced the Presidential surrender in the battle of the tapes showed a dauntless confidence that the pursuit of truth could only be aided by the capture of this explosive material. The old cracked voice quavered with joy as he spoke of the spirit of unanimity and "wonderful co-opera-tion" in the Committee that had brought the victory about. This satisfaction evidently was shared by the whole beam-ing panel. Watching them, we in the audience—or at least at my corner of the press table—had to marvel at their courage before the unknown.

The Butterfield disclosure has brought a new, tantalizing element into the Watergate probe: the promise of scientific, all but measurable certainty, which Americans, averse to guesswork—so laborious—will find it hard to set aside. Whatever reason tells us, we will keep on wanting the tapes. Even before Butterfield, American inventiveness had been busy with the problem. A do-it-yourself, home-assembly kit for obtaining the truth scientifically was being tried out by amateur Watergate investigators, using a new device on the market manufactured by a small firm in Virginia and described in a recent issue of *Newsweek*. It is a long-distance lie-detector which connects, not with a human body but with tape-recordings of a voice taken from radio, TV, or from a telephone. The PSE (Psychological Stress Evalu-ator) works like a polygraph by measuring stresses on a graph. As we weighed and judged the CREEP men in the old-fashioned, red-velvet-draped Senate Caucus Room, Watergate buffs in distant towns were plugging in their machines to home-recorded tapes of the broadcast testimony and getting similar results: among the witnesses sampled, John Dean scored highest in credibility.

A Bomb in the White House

Obviously stress is perceptible in a subject's voice, as well as in his facial expressions, hands, movements of his feet under the table. In this week's hearings, emotional stress was evident in the voices of witnesses on several significant occasions, though what a lie-detector would have made of it I don't know. Mardian's hoarse anguished cry as he told of his forced service in the cover-up: "I wanted *out!* I *couldn't* practice criminal law!" And, earlier, Kalmbach in the breaking voice of an adolescent: "I wouldn't do anything illegal. I *wouldn't.*" The sincerity was pathetic; these were sobs from the Republican heart. What was vividly present to these men's minds was their respectability.

Of course they had been involved in smelly transactions before, but on a high corporate or government level, Mardian as head of the Internal Security Division of the Justice Department ordering the burglary of J. Edgar Hoover's safe, framing "conspiracy" cases against radicals, most of which were thrown out of court; Kalmbach coming close probably to extortion in raising funds from corporations (itself against the law), and representing the President in the questionable San Clemente purchase. But corporate and government transactions did not *seem* illegal to them. With the Watergate cover-up, acting on instructions of men they said they trusted, they watched themselves sinking helplessly into the low-grade criminal world of code names, pay-offs, secret assignations, blackmail squeezes. "Quicksand," repeated Mardian, once known as Mr. Law-and-Order. No wonder their voices broke.

It did not take a PSE to register Kalmbach's misery as he told of going to see Ehrlichman for reassurance, having become worried by the peculiar, shady circumstances surrounding the innocent "humanitarian" task of paying money to the defendants' families and their lawyers. He wanted Ehrlichman to tell him whether he ought to continue. " 'John, I'm looking right into your eyes,' I said. 'I know Jeanne and your family, you know Barbara and my family. You know that my family and my reputation mean everything to me. . . . And it is just absolutely necessary, John, that you tell me that . . . it is a proper assignment.' " "And did he look you in the eyes?" "Yes, he did. . . . He said, 'Herb . . . it is proper, and you are to go forward.' "

This eye-searching, too, had a certain sincerity, in the telling—a California-style hammy sincerity based on movies. Like a number of the witnesses before the Committee, Kalmbach resembled a film actor, tall, with a deep leathery tan, so deep it might have been theatrical make-up, an aging athlete's body, a peculiar dish-face, black shingle-cut hair with a little cowlick at the crown, pale blue-green eyes with a cavernous light bringing to mind blue grottoes, green grottoes, and adding a touch of old travelogue to Ehrlichman's part in the above-described scene. The ingenuous "idealistic" Kalmbach had a fitting companion in the Keystone comedy cop Tony Ulasewicz: Don Quixote cantering in from Southern California to join up with Sancho Panza, his bag man.

The duet, as a duet, was appealing. Ulasewicz's most attractive as well as most humorous quality was his pride of workmanship. He did his job well, with resourcefulness, and the heavy Brooklyn or Bronx foghorn accent brought out the metropolitan shrewdness of the New York mentality, nasal as the old North and East River tugboats. Besides being a "character," he was redolent of Europe and the immigration saga. His name was Polish, but he might equally well have been Italian or Jewish and a cab-driver instead of a retired cop. His attitude was big-city democratic, but he also showed respect for the boss, Mr. Kalmbach, respect, above all, for Kalmbach's inexperience, which marked him as belonging to a softer breed, like a Victorian lady. Kalmbach could never have carried ten-dollar bills amounting to $50,000 around in brown paper bags tied with little pieces of string. Kalmbach would have had to put them in an attaché case and probably forgotten it on a plane. Kalmbach would never have thought of a bus-driver's metal money-changer to store coins for pay telephones (phone booth to phone booth—the only safe way); it must have been years since he had ridden on a bus.

Soon Kalmbach began to look to him for counsel. When Ulasewicz went to California for the last pick-up—$40,000 —Kalmbach met him at the airport in a rented car. "Just prior to this, I had already suggested to Mr. Kalmbach that this has definitely gone a different direction than originally anticipated." They were confronting a critical moment; back east, in Washington, Mrs. Hunt had upped her demands again. "I got in the car and Mr. Kalmbach said 'Tony, what's your opinion of all this?' And I said 'Well, Mr. Kalmbach, I will tell you, something here is not kosher. . . . It's definitely not your ballgame, Mr. Kalmbach.' "

It was easy to identify oneself with Ulasewicz in his suspense-filled adventures, which were rather like a Harold Lloyd comedy. After all, he was not trying to dispose of a

body but only of packages of money which at the beginning, as though they were dead bodies, nobody wanted to
touch. Through him, and picturing him as a partner, one
could even sympathize a little with Kalmbach.

His great moment, though, of sympathy, which he did not
play for, came toward the end of his testimony when the
panel read aloud to him a telephone conversation he had
had with Ehrlichman and which Ehrlichman, without his
knowledge, had taped. It was the day before Kalmbach was
to go before the grand jury. The conversation, in transcript,
sounds slightly garbled (or cut?); nevertheless it is clear
that Ehrlichman is directing him to lie, to cover him and
Haldeman—reminding him (in case he didn't know) that
it was Dean, *Dean,* remember now, get it straight, who was
pulling the strings. Kalmbach rather weakly agrees with
everything "John" is saying to him, but he is so over-
wrought and confused that he hardly grasps the "angle"
Ehrlichman is pushing at him. He keeps coming back to the
only point that counts for him: *Ehrlichman's* instruction
to go ahead. "Do you feel, John, calling it straight shot
here, do you feel as assured as you did . . . that there's
no culpability here?" "Yes." "And nothing to worry
about?" [Pause or something missing] "And, Herb, from
everything I hear, they're not after you." "Yes, sir." "From
everything I hear." "Barbara, you know."

Asked how he felt when he learned that Ehrlichman had
taped the call, he said as if he'd been kicked in the stomach.
Not an imaginative comparison, and he had used it before
in another context. But his very poverty of expression
awakens pity for him, as with the single word "Barbara,"

like an animal bleat of pain. In contrast we hear the cock-sure brutal voice of the man whose eyes he had searched. A master's voice impatiently coaching the poor whipped Kalmbach in the tricks he must perform before the grand jury tomorrow.

This leads a person of normal judgment to wonder why Ehrlichman made the tape and even more why he kept it and turned it over to the Committee. The tape does not incriminate Kalmbach, who is just listening and making automatic noises of assent. But it shows Ehrlichman forcefully inviting his friend to commit perjury. That is the only way it can be read. Perhaps this throws some light. If Ehrlichman cannot realize what his taped voice says in plain English, maybe that is Nixon's situation too. In that case, perhaps he can overcome his vacillation, and his own battery of tapes may be produced after all.

The
Moral
Certainties
of John D.
Ehrlichman

July 29, 1973

A "dumb, shocking, irredeemable type of thing" John Ehrlichman called it this week in his testimony. This view of the Watergate break-in has been endorsed by all the hardliner witnesses before the Senate Committee. You keep hearing it loudly proclaimed, too, in conversation whenever you meet a Nixon loyalist. It is the one thing the Ehrlichmans and Mitchells and Mardians feel strongly about—the *stupidity* of the break-in. They and their allies throughout the land do not mince words in condemning the perpetrators and sound truly outraged, as if an injury to their brains had been sustained.

Haldeman felt the same way, Ehrlichman told the senators. On June 18, the day after the break-in (an earlier, unrevealed one had taken place in May), they were talking it over on the telephone. "Both of us wondered why in the world anybody would want to break in there." From where they sat, they could see nothing in Democratic headquarters to warrant the effort: the Democratic party was just a shambles. And John Mitchell, in a civil deposition, when asked whether he had ever contemplated any form of surveillance of the Democrats, answered dryly: "No, sir, I can't imagine a less productive activity than that."

The idea that Watergate was a folly ("an unauthorized adventure by some boys with hundred-dollar bills in their pockets . . . James Bond . . ." gurgled white-haired

Richard Moore) has never been examined on its merits by the opposition, which has assumed, perhaps through sheer aversion to the Watergate dismissers, that there was something useful to the Republicans to be learned at Democratic headquarters. It was natural to do so in the first heat of argument, for to agree that it was "dumb" implied that the break-in could not be taken seriously, that being of course the White House attitude. The gravity of a violation of the law tends to be weighed in terms of the end-product. If I steal a loaf of stale bread, I may expect more lenient treatment than if I stole a Cadillac. To Mitchell and his boys, the files and telephone conversations on the sixth floor of the Watergate office building were a loaf of stale bread, so what was all the fuss about? "A ridiculous caper blown up out of all proportions." Mitchell a year later was still standing by that early press statement. It was not just CREEP that could not contain its amusement. Those bungling Cubans wearing surgical gloves! For months journalists and newscasters referred to it as the Watergate caper.

This helps to explain why the Democrats were able to do so little with the issue during the McGovern campaign. It was only when the original crime was compounded by a series of felonies and found to have been linked with other crimes—the dirty tricks department, which included the forgery of letters sent through the U.S. mails—that the gravity of Watergate became apparent.

Though the break-in, when they heard of it, struck them as loony, Haldeman and Ehrlichman nevertheless were worried. There was "a lot of concern," Ehrlichman acknowledged, that the trail would lead to the White House. Unfair, but the opposition would play it that way. "The fact that the Democrats were going to exploit it was the most important thing." Facing up to that contingency led to a number of hasty counter-measures and efforts to cover the trail that in Ehrlichman's estimation (so he let us understand) were just as idiotic as the original break-in. But nobody consulted him, naturally. When he heard that Acting FBI Director Pat Gray had gone ahead and destroyed the "politically sensitive" papers in Hunt's White House safe, he was "just nonplussed," he declared with feeling. What a dumb, shocking thing to do. Who would have thought that that was how the bonehead would interpret the instruction given him by Dean in Ehrlichman's own presence, which was to make sure nobody saw them? Gray was to take them for safekeeping, that was all.

In the same way, he still remembers his shock and surprise when he heard about the burglary at Ellsberg's psychiatrist's office. Not that it was *wrong:* he is sure (or, as he says, "shurr") that the President has the constitutional power to burglarize in the interests of national security and sure that in these circumstances a doctor-patient relationship should come under that head—no doubt of that at all. But it was so *unnecessary.* Anybody who had practiced law knew there were smarter ways of getting a patient's dossier —perfectly legal ways: working through another doctor, conning a nurse or a nurse's aide. . . . For their part, former Attorney General Mitchell and former Assistant Attorney General Mardian would not *think* of paying blackmail: it never worked; the ante just kept going up. And Mitchell knew better, he said, than to try to put a fix on a federal judge: "absolutely non-productive."

In fact, the burglary of Dr. Fielding's office proved to be non-productive too. When Hunt and Liddy broke in, presumably wearing their CIA-provided disguises, the Ellsberg file was not there. No doubt the doctor, having already been visited by the FBI, took the obvious precaution of removing the file from the premises.

The two Watergate break-ins, the cover-up activities, the Plumbers' activities (at least the ones known to the public) turned out, in the long or short run, to be totally useless in accomplishing their objects, and sarcastic men like Mitchell and Ehrlichman looked back dourly from the witness chair on the disagreeable shocks and surprises they had had on learning (usually, they claimed, from the newspapers) of the clownish, pointless actions of their associates and hirelings. A continual embarrassment. Listening to Ehrlichman, one was led to wonder whether there could be such a thing as an intelligent crime, a crime, that is, worth committing in the eyes of an intelligent person. The answer, probably, is no, though not from a point of view to which Ehrlichman would be attracted.

Perhaps he cannot help his face, but he looks like somebody of a deeply criminal nature, out of a medieval fresco: the upward sneering curl of the the left-hand side of the mouth matched, on the bias, by the upward lift of the right eyebrow, above which there is a barely discernible scar; the aggressive tilted nose that cameramen say has been growing all week, the sinister (literally) thrust of the jaw. Everything about his features and body movements is canted, tilted, slanting, sloping, askew. The arms swing loosely; the left hand with a big seal ring, like a brass knuckle, moves in a sweeping gesture. The broad head is too round—pygmyish. There is a horrible concessive little smile, like a tight parenthesis, when somebody else makes a joke.

A deformed personality, one would say, so much so that it gives one a start to hear him use the phrase "I am morally certain" in a sentence, to indicate "I am practically sure" that something or other did not happen. To Ehrlichman, most of the crimes under discussion—perjury, obstruction of justice, breaking and entering—appeared profoundly stupid and childish, above all avoidable, as legal ways of obtaining the desired result always exist. There is no reason not to believe that this is indeed his feeling, and there was no evidence on hand that he had personally committed any of them. The only crimes he could respect would be crimes wearing the mask of legality (or embodied into the statutes by an Administration with a "mandate") and crimes that are not traceable. When he put a big "E" for "Approve" on the Krogh-Young memo recommending a covert operation against the Ellsberg psychiatrist, he added "As long as it's not traceable." Confronted with the memo by the Committee, he gladly identified his handwriting; the proviso only meant, of course, that the Plumbers should not present their "calling-cards" at the doctor's office.

In handling the Watergate matter, his technique is utter disassociation. In his own mind, there is not the faintest connection between him and the actions performed by other characters in the story. Ulasewicz? He was "a facility that came with the office." Kalmbach? He had given Herb no assurances; the eye-searching (he smiled) of course never took place. He would remember it if it had. The Houdini-like power of self-extrication was so extraordinary that he actually shifted the scene of that compromising dialogue: where Kalmbach had placed it in Washington, Ehrlichman wafted it to California on a magic carpet, and none of the senators or Committee counsel noticed the landing bump.

The motive for this transfer was not obvious. Perhaps it was to avoid a perjury citation. Since he denied the content of the conversation, by referring it to another place— Kalmbach's office at Newport Beach, where they met on some different occasion—he avoided a direct lie.

In many ways his testimony with its repeated failures to recall and its little triumphant quibbles ("Did you bug that conversation?" "No, Senator, I did not." "What did you do?" "I recorded it") was very like Mitchell's. In the Caucus Room people were arguing whether he or Mitchell was more purely evil. It is hard to decide which of the two should be awarded that particular apple. Mitchell was sour, old, rancid, terse. Ehrlichman was resilient, extremely loquacious, limber as his eyebrow; he thought very fast, deflecting a question almost before it reached him, impatiently interrupting. His thinking process was a massive motor response to a set of stimuli; no instant for reflection intervened. Tilting back and forth in his chair, he resembled one of those old snap-back dolls with a very low center of gravity. In this sense, he was stupid and lump-ishly unaware of it.

The difference between him and Mitchell came down to the difference between the randy insolence of power and a surly nihilism proceeding from defeat. Mitchell is finished, a gloomy discard, but unless Ehrlichman's energetic confidence was simulated, he has no doubts about his future. He and Haldeman *are* the future, his outthrust jaw proclaimed: Watergate was a minor interruption. He is a Christian Scientist, which should not be overlooked in estimating his sense of superiority to mere matter in the form of evidence. But he is also a political animal and must estimate that Nixon's decision to tough it out with the Senate Committee and the Special Prosecutor is a winning decision. If the court blocks him and the Congress continues its petty harassment, he can govern by plebiscite, going straight to the nation for a vote of confidence in the Presidency—yes or no. One could almost see the thought shaped in Ehrlichman's broad skull. Hence his insistence on the President's constitutional power to suspend the Constitution (for that is what his arguments amounted to), which sounded bizarre, nearly crazy, in the setting of the Caucus Room. One watched Senator Ervin follow the elated, voluble reasoning, somber eyes forward, palm to cheek, almost motionless, like a Statue of Desponding Liberty.

Ehrlichman's arrogant sureness of himself, the grandiose doctrine he was enunciating of presidential powers, half-cracked or not, seemed portentous as the week went on. When all the senators rose and raised their right hands to

vote Aye on sending the case of the White House subpoenas
to the courts to compel Nixon to honor them, the room was
completely silent except for the whizzing of the cameras.
We were respecting what all felt to be an historic moment—
the kind that used to be painted and hung, in reproduction,
in schoolrooms: Washington Crossing the Delaware. It
looked as though a collision course had been set, and everyone remembered Ehrlichman's raised right hand as he took
the oath on Tuesday with a gesture one newspaper had
compared to a fascist salute.

He lost no opportunity to patronize, bully, and affront
the senators, as well as Majority Counsel Dash. The performance seemed carefully deliberated, like his opening
statement, the "high-school civics lesson" which he had
evidently rehearsed before a mirror, while shaving perhaps. Yet it did not look, at least to me, as if he were aim-
ing—over the heads of the Committee and the hostile
crowd—at an unseen TV audience. Nixon's devoted ad-
herents are not watching the hearings anyway, and as a
media-conscious man, Ehrlichman must be aware of the
national popularity of the show and of Senator Sam as a
folk hero. But his behavior with the courteous old legisla-
tor was so contumacious that the hearing-room grew turbu-
lent; there was a general incensed feeling that the senators
should not take this lying down. I slipped into one of the
reveries of the impotent and imagined the Chairman signal-
ing to the sergeants-at-arms: "Arrest that man." The sneering devil, like Iago (I daydreamed), would be hustled
out, preferably in chains, down to the old prison below the
House of Representatives where persons in contempt of

Congress used to be held. That was what he deserved, to be kicked back several eras into the antique history of the Republic. Many agreed with the thought.

On Thursday, Senator Ervin, very much in his TV character, reminded the witness of the parable of the Good Samaritan. "I read the Bible. I don't quote it," Ehrlichman muttered, very loudly, back. He can hardly have expected applause from the national TV audience for that.

If his performance was designed for an audience, its purpose at times seemed to be to frighten and overawe it, at times to disregard it utterly—itself a terror technique. He did not mind looking like a hangman. Senator Weicker, his most doughty antagonist (Ervin to our dismay appeared stricken or on the verge of an apoplectic seizure), faced him with remarks he had made about Pat Gray, a friend of Weicker's, during the Senate confirmation hearings for the post of FBI director. Gray, then Acting Director, an Honest Cop, though weak, had talked too much while being examined by the Senate and had just lost the Administration's backing. Ehrlichman was talking to Dean: "I think we ought to let him hang there. Let him twist slowly, slowly in the wind." Ehrlichman, in the witness chair, bared his teeth in brief amusement. "That was my metaphor."

Under friendly questioning, he treated himself as a highly responsible, firm-jawed civil servant, concerned with national security, relations with Congress, and general updating of administrative processes. He had stepped in to give the senators an inside view of how the shop was run. When the questioning would ramble on to Watergate or other uncomfortable topics, he would still be the pre-

occupied executive, excusing himself for not having knowledge of matters outside his immediate field or too minor to
claim his attention, saying blandly over and over, "I'm not
your best witness on that." This did not work with Pat
Gray's friend from Connecticut. "I am not your man,"
Ehrlichman told Weicker, when Weicker demanded a responsive answer to a question involving the Pentagon
Papers. "*You're* the man," Weicker thundered, like a
school-play Jehovah descending from a cloud. "You're a
good witness." Unfortunately, by this time Senator Ervin,
tired of using the gavel to quell the hissing and bursts of
applause, had announced that persons expressing approval
or disapproval would be removed from the hearing-room.

Ehrlichman's bold maneuvers to pose as a non-witness to
what was virtually a non-happening bearing the name of
Watergate had an effect, similar to the Mitchell effect, of
making the proceedings seem perfectly senseless, like the
break-in they were meant to be probing into. If you got to
the bottom of Watergate, there would be nothing, a mirage.
At the same time, though, his disparagement of Watergate
and all the futile non-productive activity leading up to it
and away from it began to raise, for the first time, a funda-
mental question: did Watergate make sense or not? If the
burglars had not been caught, would it have paid off?

Magruder had testified that Mitchell had been disgusted
by the meager fruits of the first break-in, and this, he said,
became the reason for the second. But the first break-in's
failure to deliver did not lie so much in mechanical inepti-
tude (one of the original bugs did not work) as in the nature of the project. What was to be gained from tapping

Larry O'Brien's telephone and hearing his secretary make appointments with her hairdresser? The risk of detection had to be measured against the off-chance of learning something compromising. If, unlikely as that seemed, the Democratic party had a secret strategy, they were not going to be discussing it on the telephone. O'Brien knew about taps.

The dirty-tricks department, by comparison, looked like a good investment. It was active, where the Liddy operation was passive. If the Democrats had nothing worth overhearing, Liddy's men had nothing to deliver, whereas the dirty tricksters could intervene positively in the Democrats' affairs, writing false letters, disrupting the candidates' schedules, hiring blatant homosexuals and pseudo-homosexuals to lead their demonstrations, pressing explosives on veterans-against-the-war-in-Vietnam groups. . . . It almost seems as though the Mitchell-Haldeman-Ehrlichman thesis was right: Watergate *was* stupid.

One arrives then at a mystery. Someone higher than Magruder must have approved it, and what could have been the object, if not "intelligence," of which there was so little to be gathered? Perhaps Watergate responded to a soul need of the Nixon circle rather than to an immediate utilitarian goal? A need for total control of the environment. The model may be found in the Eastern bloc countries. Listening-devices installed in offices, hotels, homes, embassies serve no directly profitable purpose but simply go on recording, like an endlessly playing phonograph, furnishing employment to a vast labor force of translators and file clerks who are the only visible beneficiaries. The very purposelessness is part of the point. The citizen can find no graspable, identifiable reason for a bug to be in his house, but he guesses it is there and feels unnerved and apprehensive, to the point where he may fear to go to bed lest he talk some nonsense in his sleep.

Now we come upon this same seeming purposelessness in the White House monitoring system. The Nixon crowd, whenever they approached the President, have been under hidden surveillance. He has been under surveillance himself, like an older person setting an example. True, only Haldeman and a few others were supposed to know, but the Polish UB does not *tell* you that they have installed microphones in your apartment. At the White House an uneasy feeling got around, evidently. Dean had told of holding a Dictaphone up to the receiver when talking to Ehrlichman from Camp David. A Boy Scout improvisation. The hearings brought to light considerable evidence of regular taping of each other by Nixon's mistrustful associates—a contagion, doubtless, from the top.

This week we heard Ehrlichman tell about sounding out Judge Byrne, who was presiding at the Ellsberg trial—on a Presidential offer to head the FBI. And what did they do when they met? At Ehrlichman's suggestion, they took a walk in a park. Just as you would do in Warsaw or Belgrade, and just as John Dean and Kalmbach did when they met in Washington to arrange the hush money payments. But what were these men so suspicious of when they sought the privacy of the outdoors? Indoors, they could scarcely have feared that Senator Sam would have planted a wheezy tape-recorder in a drawer or be listening on an aerial attached to an ancient parked car.

In the White House and at San Clemente it must have been their own people they mistrusted—with reason—either each other or a parallel apparatus in government, FBI or CIA. For men working under these conditions, the desire to extend surveillance to the opposition party would be almost automatic. No immediate gain may have been anticipated; any gleanings would have been treated as a windfall.

The Ellsberg-Fielding burglary, to which the hearings keep coming back, as though by a homing instinct, offers some illumination when set beside Watergate. There were the same personnel—Hunt and Liddy—the same failure to obtain results, the same effort to involve the CIA, apparently as a "cover," the same evident lack of sense, if the pretended aim—to protect national security—is taken as serious. The real aim, to smear Ellsberg in the press—clearly stated in the Krogh-Young memo ("How quickly do we advance to bring about a change in Ellsberg's image?") but never admitted by Ehrlichman—itself belonged more to dreamland than to current U.S. real life.

Everybody knew that Ellsberg had been going to a psychiatrist, so how could the usual details—Oedipal murder fantasies, desire to dethrone Authority—in a doctor's file have hurt him with the press? Ehrlichman, disavowing the smear intention, was not called upon to explain. Reverting, as always, to national security, he did testify lingeringly and with emphasis to the President's intense "interest in the case." "The President was really putting the pressure on us." His own self-protective interest here, obviously, was to show himself as a mere wondering instrument of the overriding Presidential will. But in his enthusiasm to make it graphic he became indiscreet. Senator Weicker: "Are you telling me you did the break-in to satisfy the President of the United States?" Ehrlichman rapidly retreated: "No." Yet for once it had sounded as if John D. Ehrlichman had been telling something like the truth.

Whoever approved Watergate may not have been conscious of any particular compelling reason for spying on the Democrats and have acted only at the behest of an ungovernable urge. The pathology suggests Nixon.

Exit Mutt, Enter Jeff

August 5, 1973

There is a standard interrogation technique that was used
by Stalin's secret police to extort confessions and is still
operative, so far as I know, with the KGB. In Vietnam,
where the U.S. Army used it to develop intelligence from
suspected Viet Cong, it was known as the Mutt-and-Jeff,
Bad-Guy Good-Guy ploy. The detainee is first roughed up,
beaten, or more ingeniously tortured by Mutt, the Bad
Guy; when this fails to produce results, owing to the subject's losing consciousness or simply refusing to say what
is expected of him, he is turned over to Jeff, the Good Guy,
who treats him like a friend, offers him cigarettes, sometimes even a short rest, and tries by persuasiveness to gain
his co-operation. The method is supposed to be highly ef-
fective, far more so than straight brutality. The prisoner is
disoriented by the change of pace, and fear of meeting Mutt
again, if he does not yield to Jeff, heightens the gratitude
felt at finding what appears to be a normal human being
in the room.

The Mutt-and-Jeff effect was never better demonstrated
than late Monday afternoon in the Senate Caucus Room,
when Haldeman succeeded Ehrlichman in the witness chair.
Ehrlichman, who had been acting like a one-man Praeto-
rian Guard cowing a womanish bunch of toga-ed senators
or like a fascist bully boy breaking up a Social Democratic
picnic, snapped shut his briefcase and strode out, pausing

in the corridor for a few assured words with the press and
television. The audience waited with a mixture of apprehension and curiosity for Harry Robbins Haldeman, who
by all accounts was going to be even more terrifying, a
crew-cut ferocious "Prussian," named by his boss in a jest-
ing moment the Lord High Executioner. We had heard a
member of his staff, the tense, thin, red-haired Gordon
Strachan, tell the panel of being waked up at four in the
morning by Haldeman calling by radio from the Presidential plane to administer a reprimand so shattering that the
half-asleep young man wondered whether it might not have
been a bad dream and telephoned the signal operator who
had relayed the call to ask, "Did I just get a call from Mr.
Haldeman?"

Before we saw Ehrlichman, we had read that he was
the weaker one of the pair and might even break under
questioning. But Haldeman, all agreed, was made of stone.
Instead, there appeared a modest figure in a rather badly
cut suit, slighter and smaller than his co-worker, bony, with
a spine that made an awkward bump in the back of his
jacket; there was something almost rabbity about him as he
slipped into his seat and respectfully faced the panel after
a quick boyish smile at someone he recognized at a nearby
table. The fearsome crew cut was moulting into baldness,
and he had rather appealing ears. Unobtrusive, unassum-
ing, deferential, he began to read a long mild statement,
incorporating in an early paragraph a list of his credentials: regent of the University of California, chairman of
the board of trustees of the California Institute of the Arts,
trustee of the Kennedy Center for the Performing Arts, and
so on.

The change of pace, so disarraying to everyone's pre-
conceptions, soon produced, as with little Jeff, a feeling
of gratitude in the public and in the viewers in their homes.
There was nothing here to fear for our liberties; this was an
unexceptionable bureaucrat dedicated to his task, perhaps
misguided in his single-minded devotion to Nixon but incapable, one would swear, of countenancing irregularity.
If he and Ehrlichman had not shared a single "mouthpiece," John L. Wilson, the dean of reactionary lawyers in
Washington, a querulous dropsical old party with a mean
City Hall mouth and a shrill ungoverned temper recalling
Rumpelstiltskin, one could not have dreamed that they had
anything in common except the fact of having served together in the White House.

True, in Haldeman's opening statement, there had been
one troubling passage under the heading "SEGRETTI," where
he itemized some actions that Segretti did *not* engage in:
"violent demonstrations and disruption, heckling or shout-
ing down speakers, burning or bombing campaign headquarters, physical damage or trashing of headquarters and
other buildings, harassment of candidates' wives and families, disruption of the National Convention by splattering
dinner guests with eggs and tomatoes, indecent exposure,
rock throwing, assaults on delegates, slashing bus tires,
smashing windows, setting trash fires under the gas tank
of a bus, knocking policemen from their motorcycles."

All these activities, in case anyone had wondered why
he was listing them, "took place in 1972—*against* the campaign of the President of the United States by his opponents. Some . . . with the clear knowledge and consent of
agents of the opposing candidate . . . ; others were acts of

109

people who were clearly unsympathetic to the President but may not have had direct orders from the opposing camp." He pointed out that there had been no investigation of these activities, "either those . . . directly attributable to our opponent or those which certainly served our opponent's interest. . . ."

This icy, murderous parenthesis, however, was followed by a few contrite words to Senators Muskie and Humphrey for the letter falsely defaming them. If Segretti "or those under his direction, as alleged," had written it, he wanted to and did apologize to both men on behalf of the whole Nixon campaign. Nothing of the kind had ever been envisioned in the instructions given Segretti.

All through Monday and Tuesday the impression was favorable. Even the low blow aimed at McGovern could be understood as fair fighting in terms of Haldeman's own belief that the country had been on the verge of civil war during the '72 campaign. Senator Ervin, mischievous: "You sound as if the country was in a state of insurrection." Haldeman, serious: "If you had been with the President, as I was, you might have thought that, Senator." It was possible that he had genuinely held McGovern responsible for a campaign of terror, not personally, of course, but indirectly through his very blindness to the real nature, so clear to Haldeman, of what some of his staff and the young people around him were encouraging. That Haldeman might be wrong in his assessment did not prove that he was a liar or a bad witness about matters, essentially bureaucratic, within his own knowledge.

Perhaps he declared a few too many failures of memory,

almost never denying outright what another witness had testified but saying "Well, I don't remember it that way" or "No, I don't think that could have happened." But this had an engaging quality. When asked how he had come to know of the Watergate break-in, he had, he said, half-smiling, "to give the most incredible answer": he honestly could not remember. That rang rather true: Gordon Strachan remembered that he was sitting in his car in front of Waterman's drugstore when he heard the news on the radio, but others, for the life of them, cannot say where they were or what they were doing when they learned some fact of great importance—an accident, a family death.

Somewhat less convincing but still within the range of possibility was that he did not remember giving Strachan an instruction on June 20, "Well, make sure the files are clean," after Strachan had reminded him of the $300,000 "sophisticated intelligence plan" memo and other compromising documents that were there. Nor any later conversation with him about it. He was sure Strachan must be wrong in his recollection. But he could not guess why Strachan would testify the way he had on that score; he had a high opinion of his loyalty, thoroughness, and veracity. There are some things you just can't explain. He can find no record of a meeting with Dean on June 23, but maybe they talked on the telephone. He thinks it was Magruder who called him on the morning of June 18, but if Magruder says *he* called *him*, he will accept that.

A spirit of conciliation shone through his testimony, not just toward the senators and counsel—conciliation toward earlier witnesses and toward the facts that had been amassed by the Committee. He was the only one of the Nixon loyalists to make an effort to sound plausible. This seemed part of the general modesty (as he showed it to us) of his nature; and the apparent modesty of his workhorse intellect, in contrast to the frightening brain power of Ehrlichman, was very reassuring. He went to meet the record half way, whenever possible, as though eager to see that his own account and the record could pull together, like a team.

The spirit of conciliation was catching. The listeners began to try to accommodate what he was saying to what they had heard before, that is, to reconcile the two. Soon even his natural enemies—liberals and skeptical newsmen—were asking themselves if Strachan, for instance, could have misunderstood him. He heard "Make sure the files are clean" and jumped to the conclusion that Haldeman had meant shred everything in that folder. But what if Haldeman, as he swore, had never looked through the file (too much paper came his way) and only Strachan knew there was compromising stuff in it? Maybe Haldeman, who had not been paying attention to his chatter about a $300,000 plan, had meant something innocent like "Get the dust off those files of yours." That way they could both be telling the truth or what each firmly believed to be true.

The desire to reconcile two seeming opposites went out to embrace Dean. Was it possible that Dean had misunderstood the President?

Knowing what he himself knew of the cover-up (just as Strachan knew the contents of that folder), he jumped to the conclusion that Nixon knew too. When Nixon com-

mended him Sepember 15 for doing a good job, Dean took
the harmless words (which could have meant only that
Nixon was glad to see that the investigation had moved
ahead swiftly) for congratulations to him for his guilty
part in limiting the grand jury indictments to the four
Cubans and McCord plus Hunt and Liddy. Perhaps every
word on the Watergate topic exchanged by Nixon and Dean
had been susceptible to a double interpretation, each mis-
reading what was in the other's mind. So that Nixon's statement, in his letter ten days ago to Senator Ervin, that the
tapes were entirely consistent with what he knew to be the
truth but were liable to misinterpretation by people with
different perspectives and motivations might be an exact
summary of the situation.

The thought was disturbing; it meant that so many of us
had been wrong. Yet it could not be dismissed out of hand.
And it allowed for the impression so many of us had had
that Dean was telling the truth. He had *thought* he was telling the truth. At so many points Haldeman's testimony
matched his. Nixon *had* said that to raise a million dollars
would be no problem. According to Haldeman, he had
added "But it would be wrong." Maybe Dean had interpreted that as a sly, winking remark made to a knowing
confederate, interpreted it, that is, as meaningless, a con-
vivial noise, and promptly let it slip from his mind.

And Dean's description of Watergate as a cancer growing on the White House. Had Dean said that, Haldeman
was asked. The audience held its breath. Reply, very calm:
yes. And the strange remark made by Nixon when Dean
had finished his account of escalating blackmail: that it

113

would be an excellent idea if Dean would brief the Cabinet on that. Yes, the President had said that but he only meant that Dean should brief the Cabinet on the fact that nobody in the White House was involved. Even one of the little things that had seemed so true to life when Dean was telling them turned up, surprisingly, in Haldeman's testimony. But it was Dean, not he, who had said it: "Draw the wagons up around the White House and let the chips fall where they may."

When Haldeman in his opening statement let out almost casually the news that he had listened to two of the White House tapes, with that single stroke, he immensely added to his credibility. The public, including the senators, burning with curiosity to know what was on the tapes, gladly seized on the only man (or so it was first thought) who had heard them. What a pity, though, that he had played only two. Why no more? It was the same as when we seize on somebody coming from the scene of a battle, a murder, an explosion, and press him for details without stopping to examine his qualifications as a witness and what bias, if any, he has. The yearning to hear the tale, not to be left out, overwhelms the critical faculty. Wanting to believe Haldeman, since we had nobody else, on the subject of those elusive tapes, we had to extend our faith to virtually the whole of his testimony. If we could not trust his word on Strachan and the files, we could not trust him to tell us what the tapes said, and when the tapes, in his version, corroborated much of what Dean had told us, the confidence we had reposed in Dean in turn corroborated Haldeman, so that for the moment they became almost equally credible as witnesses.

Thus matters stood on Wednesday morning. Only one tiny crack had opened in Haldeman's conciliating façade. In reply to a question from Dash, he mentioned a January telephone talk with Dean "when he spun out to me quite a long recitation." The sneer in the voice suddenly recalled Ehrlichman ("the most expensive honeymoon in the history of the White House"); it was Haldeman's sole indiscretion of tone. There had been a few worrying elements in the circumstances surrounding his listening to the tapes. First of all the fact that he had taken the September 15 tape home, along with some others to which he did not listen. What caused him to do that, when listening facilities were available in the Executive Office Building, where they had lent him a "courtesy" office? Well, maybe he did not want interruptions. But then there was the additional fact, which very slowly emerged, that he had left the tapes, all three or four of them (precisely how many he never said), in a suitcase in a downstairs closet for forty-eight hours, during which time, except when he returned in the evening, the house was *empty*—his wife and family had moved to California. So that an opportunity had existed for tampering with the tapes, and it did not seem improbable, after Watergate, that the White House retained a burglary "capability" somewhere on its staff.

But these were only fevered speculations, and the senators were more concerned about the propriety of Haldeman's having been allowed to listen to the tapes than about any alterations that could have been made in them while they were in his custody. They were incensed by the thought that Haldeman, a private citizen and one liable to indictment for Watergate-connected crimes, had been sent to them by the White House to give his interpretation of the "thrust" of the tapes.

Amid the general outrage and wonder at Nixon's newest *coup de théâtre*, few people tried to reassemble the pieces of the puzzle, now in sudden disorder. If Haldeman's version of the story, which asserted his own and Nixon's total innocence and ignorance, was going to prove acceptable, somebody else had to be guilty and knowledgeable. Who? Dean, as he himself acknowledged, had been an active agent in the cover-up, but he would not have undertaken that on his own. He had no motive unless he was acting on behalf of someone else. Whoever had authorized the break-in, it could not have been he.

Yet there was no time to ponder these questions. The hearings were speeding up. They started at 9:30 in the morning instead of 10:00. The lunch recess was reduced from an hour and a half to an hour, and the senators were limited to a ten-minute questioning period on each round. In the press, there was little analysis of Haldeman's testimony, and Wednesday morning he appeared to be indestructible, still modest and eager to be of service. Then his control all at once faltered, and it was on a subsidiary issue, an irrelevant issue he himself had introduced in his opening statement: the "illegal acts committed by the Democrats or serving their interest." Lowell Weicker, meditative, reread his words to him and then rapped out a question: "Exactly

which of these illegal acts do you ascribe to Senator Mc-
Govern and the Democratic party?" Haldeman swallowed.
"I am not able to do that at this time." Weicker (a Republican, remember): "Now isn't it true that the acts which
you list there didn't serve your opponents' interests, that
they did, on occasion, serve your candidate's interest?"
Haldeman, still in character: "I can't conceive of how they
did, sir."

Weicker held up a document on White House stationery,
a memo to the witness from an aide, Ronald Walker, re-
porting on the plans of demonstrators to disrupt a Billy
Graham Day celebration in Charlotte, North Carolina, at
which Nixon would be present. There would be violence
and obscene signs directed not only at the President but
also at Billy Graham. "Violence" and "obscene" and "also
at Billy Graham" had been underlined in pencil. Opposite
"obscene" somebody had written "Good" and opposite
"also at Billy Graham," "Great." It was his handwriting,
Haldeman admitted. But he could explain those notations
very easily. It was not so easy (he had only been glad, he
said, that the demonstrators would be showing their true
colors), and Weicker's ten minutes ran out.

When his turn came again, he had in hand a second
document, a memo from Haldeman to Dean dated February 10 of this year. Raising his voice and pronouncing
with great distinctness, Weicker read it. "We need to get
our people to put out the story on foreign or Communist
money that was used in support of demonstrations against
the President in 1972. We should tie all demonstrations to
McGovern and, thus, to the Democrats as part of the peace

movement. . . . This is a good counter-offensive to be developed." Haldeman acknowledged that the memo had come from him, though he had not written it; it had been put together by members of his staff from telephone calls he had had. He disavowed the "bad English" in it but stood by the contents. It was his understanding that "there were facts that led to these points." Weicker: "What are the facts?" He: "I don't know."

Soon Weicker's time ran out again, but he did not need more: the witness had been held up for public inspection twisting and squirming as he lied and equivocated. Haldeman never recovered his square, straightforward air. Before the eyes of the TV viewers, his face altered, decomposed; his eyes shifted. His mouth buttoned down, the lines around it hardening and stiffening like a buttoned-down collar. During the afternoon session that followed, he kept swallowing nervously, and his answers, increasingly evasive, showed a grim family resemblance to those of Mitchell and Ehrlichman. He was stone-walling. Good little Jeff had become Mutt—a metamorphosis. Or Dr. Jekyll was passing through some alarming intermediate stage on the way to becoming Mr. Hyde.

Meanwhile Wilson's querulous objections got shriller; you expected him to stamp his tiny foot like a thwarted Fury when overruled. Just after the blunt Weicker questioning, he made the "little Jap" remark to a reporter, who immediately released it. Last week, as Ehrlichman's counsel, he had directed a screaming tirade at the Hawaiian Senator Inouye, whose *sotto voce* comment—"What a liar!" —on his client had been overheard on television. Now he confided to the reporter that he had nothing against Weicker but could not stand "that little Jap." Fortunately for the White House (which had a spokesman and defender in Wilson), the Japanese Prime Minister, Mr. Tanaka, had ended his official visit to Washington when this made headlines.

As Senator Ervin has wearied, Weicker and Inouye have come forward as the most powerful questioners. Many people who watched on television noticed that Haldeman shrank as if afraid when confronted by the Connecticut giant, with his inherited fortune, his Republican credentials, and his copious documentation. A rumor circulates that Dean has been supplying him. Weicker and Inouye between them, in their persistent interrogation of Haldeman even before Wednesday, had uncovered fresh evidence of Nixon's true intentions for the tapes. "It was not contemplated that the existence of these tapes would ever be known"—Weicker said on Tuesday, summing up Haldeman's responses to Inouye. The witness agreed. On Wednesday afternoon, again questioned by Inouye, he reaffirmed it. If "ever" meant what it said, then the idea that had been sold to Butterfield—that they were being made for posterity—was false. *Some* explanation had to be given to the staff concerned with their maintenance and preservation, and to announce that they were being preserved as ammunition against real and potential enemies (what else?) would not have made a dignified impression. Up to now, this little disclosure has passed unnoticed by the press. Wondering whether I had heard right, Wednesday evening I turned on the television.

Inouye: What in your mind was the purpose of recording these conversations?

Haldeman: So that the President would have for his own use and reference on a historical basis an accurate and precise record of everything that was said by him and by other people with whom he was conferring.

Inouye: Was it the intention of the President to eventually release all of the tapes?

Haldeman: No, sir. My understanding was that it was he—his intention was not ever to release the tapes.

Weicker's big tilt with Haldeman and the "little Jap" story had more lively human interest than this and pre-empted most of the newspaper space. And yet if it was no great surprise to learn that Nixon had *not* been recording for posterity (though some people had actually believed that, not knowing what else to think), it was curious to hear it straight out from Haldeman.

The Wednesday morning elation soon subsided. If Weicker had routed Haldeman in single combat, something in the Caucus Room had changed, nevertheless, with Haldeman's advent. The over-winsome Senator Baker had shifted noticeably to the right, though that tiptoe move had begun the week before and may have had nothing to do with the first, favorable impact of Haldeman on the public. The climate around the senatorial table was growing stormy. A difference that had developed between the senators as to whether to prolong the hearings or pack up and go home for August suddenly took on a partisan character as a minority complained that the Democrats, by voting to defer Colson in any case till the fall, were depriving a strong Nixon spokesman of his right to be heard. Majority Counsel and Minority Counsel clashed. Senator Ervin's age was a source of anxiety to the hearers: if he went, all went, and he had not been himself since the shock (or was it a "shock" in the folk sense—a little stroke?) given him by Ehrlichman the previous week.

Meanwhile Nixon, confident, apparently, that he had found the right key, continued the "wallow in Watergate" theme; speaking at a dinner for Tanaka, he made a sidelong allusion to the "petty little indecent things that seem to obsess us," as though the indecency was of the Senate Committee's making. Hope, for the rest of us, for the country, now lay in the restorative powers of the recess. Or was shifting, like an uncertain wind, to Judge Sirica, Archie Cox, and the higher courts. Wednesday afternoon, for the first time in six weeks, I heard hisses in the room when Ervin was talking. Two small bold but discreet hisses from the back, among the standees, which were then repeated. I turned around and tried to see who was doing it, but the public looked just as usual, intent and impassive.

Always
That
Doubt

Paris. February 2–22, 1974

It is five months now since I left the Senate Caucus Room. Helms, the former CIA director, was testifying before the Committee that Thursday—thin, elegant, debonair, the only witness insouciant enough to smoke cigarettes in the witness chair. He was followed by General Cushman, who was followed, on Friday, by General Walters, both CIA brass and beefy. The next week came Pat Gray, former Attorney General Kleindienst, and Assistant Attorney General Henry Petersen, each in his own way an emotional witness, service-oriented and wearing Watergate wound-stripes. After that, the Committee went home for what was left of the summer—high time. Something had happened, probably during the Ehrlichman week, to destroy the "spirit of wonderful unanimity" of which Senator Ervin had spoken so feelingly during the early stages of the tapes confrontation. When the Committee resumed hearings in the fall, it was more disunited than ever. There have been reports and rumors of fighting within the staff between majority and minority appointees, of dissatisfaction with Sam Dash, but these internal troubles may be mere localized symptoms of a general collapse. At the height of its success, seemingly in the prime of life, the Committee behaved like a broken man, and the public was quick to sense this and demonstrate boredom. The lie put about by the Nixon people during the exciting, electrifying months of June and

125

July, that the public was fed up with the hearings and all the coverage, in due time became true.

Those who watched on television during late September (I was no longer in America) said the low point came when Patrick Buchanan, the White House speech writer, was able to make fools of the senators. For me, the low point had come before that, in the failure to call Colson to testify. Colson was a key figure, in my view *the* key figure who could have unlocked the mystery, if there really is one, of who ordered the Watergate break-ins. Though he was not Liddy's sponsor (that was Egil Krogh), he had gone out of channels to press for action on the Liddy project, back in February, when the other principals—Mitchell, Dean, Magruder—were dragging their feet. That is, if Jeb Magruder can be believed. The master of dirty tricks had called Magruder one evening "and asked me, in a sense, would we get off the stick and get the budget approved for Mr. Liddy's plans, that we needed information, particularly on Mr. O'Brien." Unfortunately for Magruder, Fred La-Rue, who he said was present during this conversation, had no recollection of it. Yet Dean accepted Magruder's word that there had been pressure on him from Colson and not just on that one occasion. Dean had the impression that Colson was on Magruder's neck. And even if one wonders about Magruder, there is the fact that it was Colson who detailed Howard Hunt, his employee and long-time protégé, to work on the Gemstone operation with Liddy and McCord, giving him time off from his own projects. Colson denied McCord's assertion that he had prior knowledge of Gemstone and was supported by Hunt in an affidavit sworn to on April 5, 1973—the last known payment ($75,000) through Hunt's lawyer, which, according to Dean, both Colson and Ehrlichman had been active in pressing for, was made on March 21. Then, appearing before the Committee in September, Hunt changed his story: he did remember one or more conversations with Colson about the Liddy plan ("his only problem with it was that he would much prefer me—to see me heading it rather than Mr. Liddy") and in fact remembered telling him back in January 1972 of his intention to recruit the same team of Cuban-Americans he and Liddy had used in the burglary of Ellsberg's psychiatrist. With the addition of the Cubans to the original nucleus, the Watergate break-in became operational.

Of all Nixon's counselors, Colson thus appears to have been not only the most zealous in pushing for Gemstone but also—a further sign of zeal—the most familiar with the mode and staffing of the operation. McCord testified that a typewritten step-by-step plan for the break-in, which Hunt showed him in his office, was being taken, he understood, to show Colson. This was more than a conjecture.

. . . at one point, he held this plan in his hands, and his words were, he interjected the name of Mr. Colson into the conversation at that point, words to the effect, "I will see Colson." And he held the paper in his hand in this sense. From that statement, I drew the conclusion that he was going to see Mr. Colson and discuss our giving him the operational plan.

If Mitchell ever got any such blueprints or was aware of a Cuban component in the personnel, no witness has been able to say so. The same with Haldeman. Nobody, not even Magruder, has claimed that the Gemstone memos Haldeman received through Strachan contained any pro- grammed "specifics." Possibly this is just a difference of temperament: Colson eager and pushy, the others prudent and incurious.

The Senate panel's excuse for not calling Colson when hearings resumed in late September was that they had heard him in executive session, where he had taken the Fifth Amendment on every question put to him. Even so, the Committee might have let the public *see* him take it, in response to counsel's questions: "I refuse to answer on the ground of self-incrimination," "I refuse to answer," "I refuse to answer," "I refuse. . . ." He would have been the only witness before the Committee to take the Fifth in open session. Liddy had invoked it in executive session, just as he had refused to take the stand in his own defense in Judge Sirica's court. In jail he has maintained his silence, though he could bargain his way out if he would talk. The Colson-Liddy axis represents the irreducible hard core of resistance to investigation of Watergate, as on another plane does Nixon himself. It would have been educational for the public to watch the spectacle (martyrdom, he would have called it) of the recusant Colson in the Caucus Room and draw the analogies.

A second (or third) low point was reached in October when Senator Ervin, summoned from New Orleans to the Oval Office, agreed to the so-called Stennis compromise, by which Nixon would give the tapes to Senator Stennis, an ancient, infirm Southern reactionary, to listen to and check against the summaries the White House would furnish the

Committee. Senator Baker, found in Chicago, agreed too, but this was not surprising since Baker for some time had been inching toward the Administration, having concluded (I would assume) that that was the winning side. The shock was Sam Ervin. Even though he soon retracted his agreement, declaring that the compromise had been misrepresented to him (he had understood that the Committee would get transcripts, not summaries, and had been allowed to think that Archie Cox had accepted the compromise), he sounded unlike himself, befuddled and vague. How could the old man, looking benign and dreamy in that Oval Office rogues' gallery, have welcomed a Trojan horse into his so long and stoutly defended territory? A country lawyer looks a gift horse in the mouth.

The answer, I am afraid, is that most men have a fatal weakness or—to stay in Troy—an Achilles heel, and Nixon had found Ervin's. Ervin is a hawk. We had forgotten or all but forgotten it in our affection for his love of liberty, Shakespeare, and the Bill of Rights. But Nixon had not. When the Stennis compromise was proposed, the Middle East crisis was at its height, a confrontation with the Soviets was looming, and the White House played on the old warrior's patriotic sentiments, emphasizing the need for national unity in the impending showdown. Ervin succumbed. Well, every good man pays for his sins, and Senator Sam paid for a lifetime of being a hawk; he was diminished in the public eye and probably in his own. The sudden loss of his heroic stature made him seem pathetic, a deflated windbag still tiresomely huffing and puffing.

Yet one would have to have a very short memory to join

the ravens dining on his flesh. The Ervin Committee served the country well in an emergency, and if it has now out-lived its function, that is hardly a reason for minimizing what it did. Rather the contrary: the proof that it served its purpose is that it is now regarded as obsolete. The accomplishments of the Committee can be measured by asking ourselves where we would be today if it had never held hearings. Nixon would be nowhere near impeachment or resignation if the tapes had not caught him in their toils, and we might never have known of their existence without the Ervin Committee—if a junior staff member, routinely questioning Alexander Butterfield, had not chanced to ask the right question. And it was a passage in John Dean's testimony before the Committee that had led Donald Sanders, the Deputy Minority Counsel, to put the question to Butterfield: Dean had got the feeling, he said, that his April 15, 1973, conversation with Nixon was being taped. Perhaps Archie Cox and his staff would have uncovered, in time, the same information, but that is not sure. More-over, without the Ervin Committee, Cox, Richardson, and Ruckelshaus would no doubt still be in place: the Saturday Night Massacre grew out of the Butterfield disclosure. In-deed, without the Ervin Committee, there might never have been a Special Prosecutor Cox to fire.

The tapes have always been the crux of the case against Nixon, and the public has always understood that, despite the pleas of liberal editorialists who begged for greater *seriousness*, concentration on the main issues, compared to which the tapes were a childish distraction, trivial sensa-tional stuff out of a whodunit. The fear that the tapes would be tampered with, based on ordinary common sense, has been with the public since the very first day. The only wonder is that they were not destroyed altogether and then declared to be "missing," like the two under subpoena that the White House now says were never made. Why eight erasures in the eighteen-and-a-half-minute gap? Why not rub the whole thing out? * Nixon believes that there is material favorable to him in what remains of that June 20 "meeting" with Haldeman, but how can scraps of a conversation exonerate him when the surrounding parts have been obliterated? The public, unlike Senator Hugh Scott, is not such a fool, which is why, as Nixon's spokesmen now state frankly, the public must never be allowed to see them.

That the pursuit of the tapes was chasing after a will-o'-the-wisp is something else. It took no prophetic gift to foresee that even if captured they would not tell us what was on them, for the simple reason that they would not be permitted to. But the handling of the sought-after tapes by Nixon and his aides has told us a great deal or, rather, has confirmed our suspicions that something here is not kosher,

---

* The hypothesis advanced in *Science* magazine—that the panel of six experts appointed by Judge Sirica failed to take account of the possibility of electrical failure of a component in Rose Mary Woods's machine—may in fact clear up this little mystery. As the author of the *Science* article, Nicholas Wade, writing in the Washington *Post* in answer to Joseph Alsop, points out, the hypothesis, even if proved right, would still leave the eighteen-and-a-half-minute gap, or continuous buzz, to be explained. How did that happen? Someone must have held the machine on "Record" for eighteen and a half minutes, thereby effecting the erasure. One big erasure, rather than eight little ones. If you accept Rose Mary Woods's explanation, that she accidentally pressed the "Record" button and kept her foot on the pedal during a five-minute telephone call, you are left with thirteen and a half minutes of unaccountable buzz.

Mr. Kalmbach, to quote Tony Ulasewicz. The handling has turned suspicion into the nearest approximation to certainty one can have outside of signed confessions by Nixon and his associates.

Of course there are still those who can believe that the tape erasures were accidental, that by bad luck the June 20 telephone conversation with John Mitchell was never recorded because the call was made on an extension not connected with the automatic recording system, that during the April 15 conversation with John Dean in the Oval Office the equipment, owing to another accident, was "malfunctioning" or had an "inadequacy." Such people will not ask why Nixon and Mitchell were talking on another extension, *i.e.*, a "secure phone," three days after the break-in: there could be a lot of innocent explanations, *e.g.*, that Nixon, when the Mitchell call came, was answering a call of nature. Yes: it makes me think of the old joke about the jealous Frenchman wanting solid proofs of his wife's infidelity: at last he catches her in bed with a lover, and his friend, to whom he relates the story, says *"Eh bien, enfin!"* but the husband shakes his head sadly—*"Toujours ce doute."* Anybody who is satisfied that the tape erasures and the missing tapes prove nothing would probably not be satisfied by Mr. Nixon's signature on a full confession and ask for handwriting tests, medical certificates stating that he had not been drugged or hypnotized. . . .

Naturally, it would be a help if Haldeman, Ehrlichman, Mitchell, and Colson—or any one of them—were to turn state's evidence, and if Nixon falls we shall certainly hear more from some of them. There will be a scramble to shift responsibility, like a football, from one member of the former team to another and back to the old quarterback, who was calling the signals. But to hope that these men, singly or in unison, will talk and bring *about* Nixon's fall is nearly as foolish as the hope that the tapes would talk. The tapes *have* talked, by now, to the maximum (one guesses) of their ability; they have told us that someone with access to them—and that cannot be John Dean—is afraid of them. But then Haldeman, Ehrlichman, Mitchell, and others have also talked; we heard them before the Ervin Committee proclaim their guilt by open equivocation and manifest lying. Though they left us to speculate on the *degree* of guilt in each case, they all plainly told us that they were afraid that the knowledge they carried inside them would inadvertently slip out.

The great service of the Ervin Committee was to show these men to the nation as they underwent questioning— something that would not have been possible in a court of law, where TV is not admitted. That the questioning was not always of the best, that leads were not always followed up, is minor in comparison. The self-righteous, pedantic tone adopted by some mournful analysts writing in liberal magazines, the triumphant pouncing on sins of omission committed by the hard-worked senators are unpleasant re-minders of the persistent puritanism and Zeal-of-the-Land Busyness in our national character. The Ervin Committee was not out to convict the witnesses before it, to nail down their testimony with expert ringing blows, but to give us a basis for judging them and the Administration they served. Who can deny that it did that?

What emerged from the hearings and emerges even more clearly from the transcripts as they are published, with appendices (eight volumes now), by the Government Printing Office is an overwhelming case for impeachment and conviction. To my mind, there can be no doubt that Nixon himself ordered Watergate and was kept informed of the cover-up, which of course he did not need to order—as the testimony repeatedly brought out, the necessity of a cover-up was taken for granted as soon as news of the arrests reached the Nixon organization. Nobody had to order it; it happened by itself and was inherent in the break-in. A covert operation is covered before it gets off the ground, and the process continues mechanically to the bitter end, which is where we seem to be now. The mystery is not in the cover-up—who took part and how. They *all* took part, each in his own capacity: the money-raisers raised money; the petty bureaucrats shredded; the big bureaucrats got on the telephone to switch off the FBI investigation. Everybody (with two exceptions) stood ready, if called upon, to commit perjury; nobody talked. The mystery lies in the original decision— who made it and under what circumstances?

Without prejudgment, let us tick them off. *Mitchell*. He is the White House candidate, but that does not entitle us to rule him out of consideration. In favor of the Mitchell hypothesis is the fact that he was in charge at CREEP, out of which the conspiracy operated. Nobody in CREEP but he had the authority to order it—certainly not his deputy,

Magruder, acting on his own. And, according to Magruder, Mitchell did order it, at Key Biscayne, on March 30. The date, if not the fact, is confirmed by other testimony. According to McCord, early in March the operation had not been funded; roughly a month later it was. All through March McCord was weighing the decision of whether or not to accede to Liddy and sign on; it took him thirty days to make up his mind, and during these same thirty days (Liddy told him) ". . . the whole matter was being considered and reconsidered by Mr. Mitchell." Robert Reisner, Magruder's deputy, remembers Magruder saying to him, "Call Liddy and tell him it is approved." He is uncertain of the exact date but feels it must have been around the end of the month since Magruder gave Liddy the first two weeks in April to get ready. Gordon Strachan, Haldeman's deputy, says Magruder reported to him on March 31 or April 1 that a $300,000 "sophisticated intelligence-gathering plan" had been approved at Key Biscayne. Just before or just after April 7, according to Hugh Sloan, Liddy came to him with a sheet of paper representing a $250,000 budget on which he would soon be wanting "substantial cash payment." All this argues that if the decision was not made at Key Biscayne on March 30 (LaRue says it was not), it was made within the next day or two, and who could have done that but Mitchell?

Yet it does not sound like Mitchell. Magruder and Dean, who had been present at the two earlier meetings, both described Mitchell's very negative, pipe-puffing responses. At Key Biscayne, he was still "reluctant" (Magruder), "not enthusiastic" (LaRue). Gemstone in any of its avatars was not in Mitchell's style. Dean says the Attorney General "was not interested at all" in its predecessor, Operation Sand-wedge, when it was presented. Nor can that dour realist have cared much for Liddy, an exotic product of Ehrlichman's brain work. Liddy and his plan were a bitter pill he had to swallow and, in the hearing-room, almost visibly spat out. McCord, who was not privy to the ins and outs of Gemstone's reception, gave his estimate of how it must have gone.

I knew from previous contact with him that he was a very decisive man, that he did not agonize over decisions, and yet apparently he took this one under careful consideration and considered it for some thirty days in making the decision, and frankly, I had it, my conclusion was that he took it as well to higher authority and got a final approval from his superior before embarking on this task.

Again the sense of duress. Despite Mitchell's insistent denials, there is plenty of evidence to show that he was aware of Watergate before the morning of June 17, whether or not he had approved it, but everything points to a disgruntled, unwilling awareness. And the new awareness, coming to him late last March, of his now being set up as the "goat" for Watergate, must have increased his bile. If of all Nixon's counselors, you were the one who was a hold-out on Watergate, what a mockery, what an irony to sit in exile and bitterly savor. In the Caucus Room, he was steeped in irony, like some horrible dark and yet congenial decoction brewed in his private still. If, against his better judgment, he did authorize Watergate, he evidently had not conceived it.

Dean. He did not have the authority, and all the arguments against Mitchell's having been the "father" of Watergate would apply to Mitchell and Dean working together. If somehow he was behind Gemstone, pushing the plan forward despite Mitchell's resistance, it must have been as somebody else's representative and courier—in his characteristic messenger role. But what powerful figure could have deputized him to flit behind the scenes? His chief friend, Krogh, had no more power than he. Against Dean, however, is the fact, heavily underlined by Senator Gurney and Minority Counsel Thompson, that he had "recommended" Liddy to Mitchell, "introduced" him to the Committee to Re-elect. True, he had accompanied Liddy on his maiden appearance at the CREEP offices, and, true, he had recommended Liddy to Mitchell for the post of General Counsel. But he was only passing on his friend Krogh's recommendation, and the transfer of Liddy to CREEP had been approved by Ehrlichman when Dean brought him to the office and introduced him to Magruder, his new boss. Unlike Dean, Ehrlichman had previous experience with Liddy, having kept him on his staff and used him (with Hunt) for the burglary of Dr. Fielding's office. Ehrlichman hated Mitchell and vice versa.

Two other counts against Dean as the author or main abettor of Watergate should be mentioned. First, the fact vouched for by Magruder (and by Magruder only) that in the fall of '71, before the advent of Liddy, "some people in the White House" had been keen on an intelligence-gathering project: when asked to specify, the only name he could remember was John Dean. Finally, Dean had urged Magruder to try to stay on terms with Liddy after a falling-out. Dean did not deny this, but it scarcely constitutes proof of eagerness on his part to bring Watergate to fruition. He was a natural smoother-over, and, in any case, Strachan testified that Dean had been acting on Haldeman's instruction.

At worst, these small "damning" facts only show that Dean had more prior information about Watergate than he has admitted to. They might also show, however, that Dean, from the start, was being used as the unconscious agent of other people anxious to remain invisible: if the Liddy project went sour, only Dean could be seen as instrumental in recommending it, performing the right introductions, smoothing its course. . . .

Haldeman and Ehrlichman. Either or both had the power —if not technically the authority—to override Mitchell's objections and direct Magruder to proceed with Gemstone. Or Haldeman alone, invoking the Presidential sanction, could have forced the recalcitrant Mitchell to initial the budget; from Ehrlichman, Mitchell would probably not have accepted that. There is a faint possibility, which gets some tenuous support from Robert Reisner's testimony to communications between Magruder and Liddy, that the operation had *already* been approved by somebody not Mitchell when Magruder flew down to Key Biscayne, in others words that Mitchell's signature was a formality that could be dispensed with if need be. Yet Gemstone, at least to my mind, does not sound like a conception that could have originated with Haldeman and Ehrlichman, though it is closer to their spirit than to Mitchell's.

Even if it could not be traced to them in the event of failure, they would surely have had their doubts about the public-relations aspect of such an adventure, were the press to get hold of it. A simple CIA workhorse like Jim McCord could be persuaded that a break-in at Democratic National Committee headquarters was in the interests of national security, but Haldeman and Ehrlichman, whatever their private convictions, would scarcely have seen national security as a plausible public defense for a job against the opposition party. There is very strong evidence that Haldeman, at least, knew that a plan for electronic surveillance was in the works, but knowing and advocating are not the same thing. Probably he and Ehrlichman, assuming they both knew, kept their fingers crossed throughout May and early June. If the operation got results, so much the better; if it failed, old John Mitchell would be left holding the bag. Apprehension, on their part, must have mingled with amusement—the amusement anticipating Mitchell's grim predicament if Liddy's men got caught. This would account for Haldeman's "mellow mood" on the morning of June 20 when he checked into the office, fresh from Florida, where he had been during the break-in. Gordon Strachan went in to see him, "scared to death," fully expecting to be fired for having failed to reach his boss over the weekend and report to him on Magruder and the Gemstone connection. Instead, Haldeman greeted him "half jokingly" with "Well, what do we know about the events of the weekend?" and calmly perused the file Strachan handed him.

Colson. More likely, in all but one respect, than any of the preceding. When he heard of the break-in on his return from the Philippines, Dean's first thought, he testified, was "Colson." Asked to explain that reaction, he mentioned the Brookings Institution burglary by fire-bombing—a typical Colson project that he himself, by flying to California, had managed to avert. In addition, he had remembered Colson's friendliness with Hunt. Dean was not the only member of the White House staff to have the name "Colson" rise out of the cloudy incident like a genie issuing from a bottle. Ehrlichman, on the telephone, as soon as Dean got back to his desk in Washington, Monday morning, the nineteenth, told him "to find out what Colson's involvement was in the matter." If that instruction was given in good faith and not merely placed on the record, it shows that Ehrlichman, far from being on the inside track about Watergate, was guessing like anybody else. In any case, it was an easy guess. After being debriefed by Liddy, Mardian thought so too. On its face, Watergate looked like pure Colson.

There was only one catch: did he have the power to authorize it? The call to Magruder urging him "to get off the stick" seems to prove that he did not. That was an entreaty, not an order. The best Colson could do for Gemstone was to keep after Magruder in the hope that it would go through. If he was the master-mind, he must have had an ally more powerful than himself who interposed to put an end to shilly-shallying.

Nixon. By elimination, we arrive at the only suspect who had the power to authorize Watergate and character traits to match. Unless we say "Nixon," we are forced to conclude that nobody authorized Watergate, that the directive to fund Liddy and his co-conspirators came to Magruder from a supernatural agency, identified by some with Mitchell, by some with Haldeman, by some with Colson, and by Mitchell probably with the President.

It remains to try to analyze how and by what stages and through whom the Presidential will was implemented. Here we are in the dark, and Dean, our only guide, is in the dark too. He does not know where the plan for electronic surveillance of the opposition party (as opposed to traditional spying) originated and he offers no conjecture.

Something happened, he thinks, between December 10, 1971, when Liddy went to work at CREEP, and January 27, when he showed his charts on an easel in the Department of Justice, with Mitchell, Magruder, and Dean watching in utter astonishment. The plan for intelligence-gathering on demonstrators discussed at the time of Liddy's hiring, to occupy only a small part of his time (2 to 5 per cent, Hugh Sloan understood), had undergone a wondrous change. In the January 27 plan, the demonstrators are still there (to be kidnapped and held in Mexico till the Republican convention, then slated for San Diego, was over), but the main activity, inflated and grandiose, with a bugged yacht, call girls, and blackmail, now centers on the Democratic convention at Miami. In the scaled-down second presentation of February 4, the demonstrators have disappeared, and instead, as a sideshow to the big anti-Democratic attraction, there is a burglary of Hank Greenspun's safe in Nevada with a Howard Hughes plane standing by to fly the burglars to a Central American haven once the job is completed. In the final, Key Biscayne ver-

sion, again no demonstrators, and nothing more is heard
of them as the Watergate scheme develops except as *justi-
fication* given to McCord and the Cubans for entering
Democratic headquarters to plant bugs on telephones and
photograph papers. The Latin-American theme (perhaps
Hunt's leitmotiv) persists, though *pianissimo:* in the end
it is just money that is spirited to Mexico to be laundered.

Thus the rational basis for Liddy's employment was
quickly subordinated to irrational elements and soon van-
ished from sight. For the Republicans to be concerned
about having their convention broken up by demonstrators
(as had happened in Chicago to the Democrats in 1968)
was perfectly natural and even sensible; to infiltrate anti-
war groups would be Standing Operating Procedure and
an old habit with the FBI. That Nixon was unwilling to
leave the handling of left-wing protesters to the FBI and
the police was not quite so sensible but understandable, in
view of his feud with J. Edgar Hoover and his general dissatisfaction with the ordinary repressive agencies of government. He wanted his own spies, paid by his own
campaign people and under their supervision. What is
strange is that once this function was added to CREEP's
administrative structure no more heed was paid to it, and
it was allowed to atrophy, as though the expensive charms
of electronic surveillance were too wonderful to be wasted
on dime-a-dozen left-wingers. With the dynamic Liddy and
his vision in the pay of CREEP, somebody, singular or
plural, was tempted to divert this "capability" from powerless anti-war groups—who were only a nuisance—to the
still powerful opposition party. In this broader perspective,

the demonstrators were even seen to have a certain utility, particularly if they could be linked to the Democrats. Dean, a reasonable and pacific young man who well understood the realities of the demonstrator problem (he had won credit as a Justice Department negotiator with the leaders of the big protest march on Washington in 1969), was baffled by the sudden delusion of grandeur implicit in the Liddy charts. Mitchell, for his part, on each presentation, kept growling, in effect: "What about the demonstrators? What about our security? Why isn't this fellow working on that?"

Several times in his testimony, Dean returned to the incredible transformation that, in the space of a month and a half, had overtaken a project with which he thought he was familiar. "That has always been one of the great mysteries to me, between the time he [Liddy] went over there . . . what happened between December 10 and January 27, and my conception of what his responsibilities were and possibly his own or others' conception dramatically changed." His mystification continued and embraced the whole sequence of events right up to June 17. He had thought the plan was dead after January 27. When it resurfaced on February 4, he was alarmed enough to go to inform Haldeman. After this, he was told no more of Gemstone till he was called upon for his services in the cover-up: "I have never been clear on what happened between February and June 17." All he could say was that "someone wanted the operation."

Obviously this puzzlement of his may be specious. While admitting large responsibility in the cover-up, he may want to dissociate himself in so far as he can from the planning of the break-in. That possibility must be kept in mind, and yet it seems undeniable that on January 27 both he and Mitchell were taken completely by surprise. Could they have been deceived from the outset as to Liddy's functions? Was "intelligence-gathering on demonstrators" a cover under which the former Plumber was slipped into Mitchell's territory, with Dean, all unknowing, acting as his escort? The idea of electronic surveillance may have been in the White House air throughout the fall of 1971—the offspring of group-think with no acknowledged paternity—and Liddy may have been chosen and sent over to CREEP to try it out on Mitchell. When Mitchell refused, then the pressure slowly built up, White House desire for the project mounting as frustration was encountered.

The only evidence, though, for such a supposition comes from Magruder. According to him, Liddy, early in December, on his first days at work, was already talking of a $1 million broad-gauged intelligence plan that had White House approval. But of all the witnesses before the panel the self-seeking Magruder is the most suspect, and in any case Liddy may merely have been boasting. The "something" that happened between December 10 and January 27 (assuming Dean is right that a new factor then entered) may have been simply Liddy. He had found, ready to hand, guarded by Sloan and Porter, the pot of gold at the end of his dream rainbow. CREEP's campaign money, seemingly unlimited, may well have been the stimulus that set his brain working (who but he could have named the operation "Gemstone"?), and even before his charts had been submitted to Mitchell he had discovered a receptive audience back in the White House.

It is not hard to accept Dean's puzzlement as genuine. Both he and the unimaginative Mitchell lacked the quality of "vision" and were incapable of grasping that what had been added to CREEP with the accession of Liddy was a new potential for transforming cash into power. In the unexplored field of electronics as a campaign accessory, Nixon and his corporate backers would have a clear advantage, almost a monopoly, since the Democrats were in no position to finance million-dollar bugging experiments, so poor in fact that they were defenseless against enemy bugging—Larry O'Brien guessed that his headquarters were being tapped but could not afford to hire his own team of experts to find and de-activate the bugs. Dean and Mitchell, thinking along traditional lines, were too shortsighted to see that this unique advantage, which could outweigh the Democratic numbers (the country was still basically Democratic), should not be lightly discarded because of the risk-element. Liddy ought to be given a trial, an initial dry run, to show what he could deliver. Unable to look at it that way, with an open mind, they were at a loss when Liddy appeared, apparently as a missionary from some quarter, undiscouraged by orders to "burn that stuff," obediently cutting down his budget requirements (as though the price-tag was the problem), and indefatigably proselytizing, like a Jehovah's Witness who has got one foot in the door. Who had sent him, what could be behind him, they hardly dared speculate.

And yet "someone wanted the operation" or, in Mitchell's

The Mask of State

idiom, "somebody obviously was very interested." At Key Biscayne, the former Attorney General must have drawn a terrible conclusion: it could only be Nixon. Hence his spleen and misery. He was frightened by the project, frightened by Liddy, and frightened by the advice the President evidently was getting from an undetermined familiar. His suspicions must have veered angrily back and forth between Colson and Haldeman, touched on Ehrlichman and reluctantly withdrawn. Since he has the primal virtue of loyalty, he would not have let himself blame the President: those damnable others had got at him.

He may have been told, straight out, and still half-refused to believe. One can imagine the telephone call to Florida, say on March 31. Haldeman: "The President wants this, John. I sympathize with your reservations, but what can we do? He *wants* it." Or else Colson: "John, get your ass moving. That's an order from You-Know-Who. If you don't like it, put Jeb on it." Mitchell, setting down the receiver, was maybe trying to persuade himself that the caller was lying—pretending to speak for the President but really pushing his own merchandise. In that case, why not ask to hear it from Nixon directly? But that was something Mitchell was not going to risk. As long as he did not *ask* the President, he could retain a doubt. It may even be true that to this day he has refrained from asking. His categorical statement that he never discussed Watergate with the President, which the senators found inconceivable, was quite possibly a fact, though the reasons he gave (the "White House horror stories," "lowering the boom," and so on) were obviously fictitious. As so often happened in

146

his testimony, Mitchell's weary lies and justifications did not seek to convince, which was perhaps astute on his part: if the senators did not believe his explanations, they did not believe the astonishing fact he was stating, which from his point of view was just as well.

To go back to Key Biscayne. When Mitchell recognized, before, during, or after the March 30 meeting, that he could not stop Gemstone, he capitulated. But not gladly. His "I am tired of hearing it . . . let's not discuss it any further" (if that is what he said to Magruder) defined his position. His lack of stomach for the enterprise was evident in his subsequent behavior, which, stopping just short of total non-co-operation, must have appeared strange to others in the CREEP office. He left Magruder in charge of whatever Liddy was up to and gave him sole authority over the moneys dispensed to him. When Hugh Sloan, worried, begged Finance Chairman Stans to get Mitchell's sanction for the first outsize payment ($83,000) on what Liddy said was an approved $250,000 budget, Stans drew a laconic answer: "Tell him to ask Magruder. He has the responsibility." It was after this colloquy that Stans told Sloan, who wondered what the money was for, "*I* don't want to know, and *you* don't want to know." Mitchell swears he never saw the Gemstone material placed in his file by Magruder. If "never saw" means "never looked at," that may well be true. It would be Mitchell's way of demonstrating that he knew in advance (and he was right, apparently) that the material would be worthless.

If the spongy surrounding tissue of lies can be cut away (which is now possible for a reader of the transcript), much of the testimony by Mitchell and about him becomes believable. Once you accept the hypothesis that Mitchell knew (or feared) that Nixon had ordered Gemstone, nearly everything falls into place. Even his dour jests about wishing that he had shot certain people, wishing that he had thrown Liddy out the Department of Justice window. The trouble was, he couldn't, but those are the wishes you entertain, cheerful murder dreams, when you sit by yourself, powerless, watching the fools take over. His exclamation (reported by LaRue) on getting the news of the break-in—"This is incredible!"—sums up with explosive sincerity his feelings on the subject or, as he would say, on the subject matter. Incredible from the beginning and incredible in the finale. That they should have let themselves get caught was predictable, but that *McCord* should have been with them! The CRP security officer! It blew your mind.

Mitchell testified that he had taken no part in the cover-up. Few believed him, but it was probably half true and it expressed a whole truth of feeling: he *wanted* no part of the cover-up. Probably he had as little faith in the abilities of the cover-up activists as he had had in Liddy's capacities. John Dean had sparks of judgment, but he was busy being a messenger boy for the others. Mitchell trusted only his own people: Mardian and LaRue. And to be forced to cover up for a crazy action that you had opposed from the outset was a bit much. In trying to cover up, you might be digging yourself in deeper. Yet there was his loyalty to the President to remember, there was the election, and there was the fact that the faithful LaRue was being dragged into the business of paying hush money to the defendants while Mardian had been drafted into the role of Liddy's legal adviser, among other uncongenial Watergate-related tasks. Under the circumstances, Mitchell could not refuse to lend a hand. Though his opposition to Gemstone had probably cost him the President's friendship, he carried on.

He seems to have drawn the line, though, at hush money. Somebody, no doubt, had to pay it, but let them use White House funds and not come to him about it. The last time anyone tried to enlist his help in the pay-offs was in February 1973 when his old friend Richard Moore was dispatched to New York by Haldeman and Ehrlichman, in the unlikely hope that Mitchell could be persuaded to raise money for "lawyers' fees" from "his rich New York friends." Mitchell's answer: "Tell them to get lost." On March 21, LaRue was worrying about a $75,000 payment he had been directed to make to Hunt's lawyer. This was a large sum, the largest he had paid out yet, and he hesitated to use his own judgment on whether or not to make the delivery. Dean was not helpful and suggested that he call Mitchell, which LaRue did. "He told me that he thought I ought to pay it." This can be construed as authorization (Mitchell, then, making an exception to the sour rule he had set himself) but it can also be construed as philosophical advice given to a distraught old friend who had come to him for counsel: "Well, Fred, it looks to me as if you'd better pay it. They've got you by the balls." What they did with that White House slush fund was not Mitchell's lookout: LaRue would be drawing on a $350,000 under-cover

149

cash reserve that Haldeman had been holding in an office safe to be used "for polling purposes."

Yet for all his disgust and rancor, Mitchell, being human, must have blamed himself as well as the others for the Watergate fiasco. Against any nominee but McGovern, it could have cost Nixon the election, and Mitchell, in that eventuality, would have had plenty of cause for self-reproach. If he had not stubbornly declined to know anything about Gemstone, if he had not left it strictly to Magruder, in short if he had not been so unyielding, the burglars might still have been caught, but there would have been no Jim McCord among them. Nor, if Mitchell had had any say, would a White House telephone number have been found in two of the Cubans' address books or sequenced CRP bills in their pockets. So, at any rate, he may have argued "in hindsight," and here another bit of his testimony suddenly fits into the puzzle and assumes a truthful look. On June 20, he spoke with the President, for the first and only time, about Watergate. You could hardly call it a discussion, since Mitchell was talking and Nixon was listening. Mitchell says he apologized to the President for not running a tighter ship: "I think I made it quite clear to him that I hadn't exercised sufficient control over the activities of all the people in the Committee." That this was *all* Mitchell had to say on the matter to the Chief Executive struck most people as unbelievable, positively grotesque. Yet it was about all he *could* say in the circumstances: he was sorry he had not kept his eye on Gemstone, sorry he had left Magruder to handle it, sorry he had let his opposition to the project get the better of him. . . .

The tape of that conversation is "missing," but we can assume that Nixon's response was icy. No wonder the call was short.

If we accept that the impetus for Watergate came from Nixon, still it must have been communicated through a channel or channels. Someone besides Nixon was active in promoting the plan. Mitchell in his testimony threw out a few morose hints as to who that might have been, but he would not be more definite. "You can almost take your pick of quite a number of such influences." The obvious choice is Colson. Magruder is a possibility, though mainly because of his eagerness to divert suspicion elsewhere—onto Colson, among others. He authorized the funds, without reference to Mitchell, and he was very much up-to-the-minute on the break-in program. When Liddy called him, on the morning of June 17 in the Beverly Hills Hotel in Los Angeles, he came back from the telephone to the breakfast table and said in an aside to LaRue, "You know, I think maybe last night was the night they were going into the Democratic National Committee." But if he was getting orders from the Oval Office and feeding information back, it seems inconceivable that somebody was not acting as liaison—impossible to picture Nixon stepping into a pay phone booth, depositing a dime, and asking for "Jeb." But this sends us back to wondering about Haldeman; Magruder was a Haldeman favorite.

From some of Dean's notes written at Camp David and from remarks he made to the President, it sounds as if for a time Dean had suspected Gordon Strachan of being the principal agent or intermediary. But either this suspicion had been dropped in his ear by Magruder (status rivalry: he had been Strachan's boss in Haldeman's office and now at CREEP he was getting orders from him), or "Strachan" was a pseudonym for the big boss, Haldeman, since of all the figures we have been discussing the thin high-voiced Strachan was the most powerless. But by the time of the hearings Dean had dropped Strachan or "Strachan" and seemed to be inclining toward Colson. One wonders whether, by now, the thought of Nixon as the prime mover is turning over in his mind.

Colson, Haldeman, Haldeman, Colson—the Moving Finger writes and, having writ, erases; the needle wavers; maybe the daisies can tell. It is a count-out game. But one thing is sure: Nixon cannot be counted out. Senator Baker's "searching" question, "What did the President know and when did he know it?" could not be more incongruous. Ask when an arch-conspirator first heard of his conspiracy or when our wicked Creator got news of this wicked world.

Nevertheless, it is worthwhile to examine the circumstances out of which Watergate emerged. The crucial date was probably June 1971. The publication of the Pentagon Papers was a turning point for Nixon. At that moment, maybe at that instant, he went around the bend, from normal politics (however dirty and ruthless) to the politics of irrationality. There had been premonitory signs. Already, in the spring of 1971, the installation of the White House monitoring system pointed in the direction of Watergate, and the Huston internal-security plan of the summer of 1970 was another road-indicator. Both of these measures were well-guarded secrets, and it was Watergate, significantly, that finally released them, along with a great deal of other material that had been kept from public scrutiny. The monitoring system and the Huston plan were directed, in their different ways, at a much tighter policing of the environment and both were designed to make use of modern, up-to-date technology. An infatuation with the latest technology apparently went hand in hand with a passion for secrecy: according to John Dean, Tom Huston (whose hero was Cato the Younger) had a scrambler telephone locked in a safe beside him—he sounds like a more highly educated Liddy, a flamboyant conservative militant responsive to the appeal of space-age gimcrackery.

But the Huston plan had to be scrapped (or to go more deeply underground) after only a few days of service, owing to the resistance of J. Edgar Hoover, and this thwarting of the Presidential will occurring within the extended "family" of government must have made Nixon keenly aware of his nuclear isolation. Just as he was moving to establish the rigid control he deemed necessary to the process of governing, he was forced to note, and not for the first time, his inability to control or discipline the agencies that were supposedly under him.

He was isolated, pent up, in the White House with his tiny nucleus of planners and visionaries, and against him were allied the inert and—from his point of view—reactionary forces of the nation: J. Edgar Hoover, Helms at the CIA, the Eastern Establishment press, the judiciary, most of the Congress, and the Internal Revenue Service, manned by Democratic holdovers who blocked all his efforts to enforce legitimate authority through tax audits and tax harassment.

It is important, I think, to realize that Nixon saw nothing wrong in the conception of governing through tax harassment of foundations and individuals. To him, control of the IRS was one of the natural perquisites of the office, like the patronage dispensed by the Postmaster General, the parceling out of contracts and Embassy assignments as rewards to campaign contributors. As for the wire-tapping of dissenters and subversives, some people, he knew, thought it was illegal, but it was not *wrong*. And why shouldn't the CIA lend a hand in under-cover operations against domestic radicals? Its charter from Congress specified foreign intelligence work only, but it was common knowledge that a lot of those radicals were working for foreign powers.

Yet these little natural innocent things (how could a tax audit hurt anybody who had made an honest return?) were being treated as if they were *crimes* by the people over at IRS and by Hoover and Helms, who got legalistic when asked to do the slightest favor. It had not been that way when the Democrats were running things. The difference was Richard M. Nixon. Elected by the popular will to the highest office of the land, the President of the United States was thrust into the position of a conspirator if he was going to execute his mandate.

A number of presidents—*e.g.*, Roosevelt, Lyndon Johnson—have not been strangers to this feeling and have acted accordingly. It is probably in the nature of things that the Chief Executive will chafe against the laws and institutions restraining him more than the average citizen and turn, on occasion, into the Chief Lawbreaker. But no Administration before Nixon's can have lent itself so readily to a conspiratorial view of government. His secretive and unsociable nature made friends with the underground methods he felt were imposed on him by an unsympathetic Congress (even his own party had its Javitses and its Percys) and an un-co-operative entrenched bureaucracy. In 1970, conspiracy (the wrong kind) was much in the Administration's thoughts. At Justice, Mitchell and Mardian were bringing dissenters to trial under the conspiracy statutes and creating more dissent among the judiciary, which complained of loosely drawn indictments, tainted evidence, and the violation of the rights of defendants. From the Administration's point of view, those aborted trials should have been seen, nevertheless, as a qualified success; like tax audits, they constituted a harassment, very costly of both time and money not only to those indicted but also to their supporters, busy raising funds, writing letters to the press, hiring halls, drafting appeals. But Nixon was dissatisfied.

(A) With the judiciary and (B), probably, with Mitchell and Mardian. As he drew closer to the notion (unnamed by him, of course) of forming a conspiratorial nucleus within his own government, he began to draw away from his old counselor Mitchell, who believed in "working within the system" by rapping on the right doors. The Senate's rejection of Haynsworth and Carswell—Mitchell's nominees for the Supreme Court and part of "the Southern

155

strategy"—must have produced the first signs of a chill
on Nixon's part. Trying to work within the system, twisting
a few arms (Senator Margaret Chase Smith's, for instance),
had caused him two public humiliations and anyway it
was too slow. An analogy with the politics of the Left comes
to mind: the younger ideologues and actionists of the White
House inner circle were revolutionaries, while Mitchell and
his cronies (I ask Willy Brandt's pardon) were Social Democrats. Both had the same goal—the rule of Nixon—and the
differences were over methodology, but Mitchell's addic-
tion to the old semi-legal methods, a habit he could not
shake, was starting to prove, at least to Nixon, that he did
not understand the goal any better than J. Edgar Hoover
or Randolph Thrower of the IRS.

The disclosure of the Pentagon Papers brought all this
to a head. Their publication inflicted a *symbolic* injury on
Nixon. Whatever disapproval he was bound to express in
public, privately he might almost have enjoyed it. The
documents had nothing to do with him and cast discredit,
to put it mildly, on his Democratic predecessors. Nor did
the Pentagon come out well, which could have given him
some satisfaction; relations, as we now know, were strained
to the point where the Pentagon was spying on him. It is
understandable that he should have been led to worry about
leaks from his own Administration. Perhaps almost any
president in his place would have formed something like
a Plumbers' unit to make doubly sure this did not happen
to *him*. But Nixon's reaction of fury was far in excess of
the cause and unaccounted for by his practical interests. He
became obsessed with Ellsberg—a spaced-out academic

who would never see the inside of a government office again. By all accounts, Nixon could not get his mind off him and talked about him incessantly. Ellsberg was the goad that spurred his thinking along security lines, and the White House staff was aware of it, so much so that a sycophant like Colson, trying to keep pace with that thinking, actually directed a White House employee to set off a fire-bomb in the Brookings Institution in order to effect an entry and steal some documents they were using for a current study of Vietnam affairs. It is interesting that this project was a mirror image of the Pentagon Papers "theft," with arson, property damage, and possible loss of life added.

Nixon's determination to see Ellsberg punished, like a close personal enemy, hardened throughout the summer. All his grudges and grievances now had a point to center on: his hatred of the press, his hatred of reds and pinks, his hatred of Hoover, his mistrust of the CIA and impatience with the judiciary. The FBI was refusing to conduct a serious investigation because of a friendship between Hoover and Ellsberg's father-in-law; the CIA "psychological profile" of Ellsberg was derisory; the judge hearing the case naturally could not be counted on, so he had to be "fixed" with an offer to head the FBI.

Like furniture being moved into place to set a stage, Hunt and Liddy that summer were brought onto the White House staff. Caulfield and Ulasewicz, both with police backgrounds of investigating dissidents, were already there. Caulfield, a former Bronx cop, had been hired by Haldeman; his specialty had been "monitoring" terrorists, the Communist party, Cuban militant organizations, and "a variety of Latin domestic revolutionary groups who planned or were suspected of planning various kinds of unlawful activities." The burglary of Ellsberg's psychiatrist was coming.

The Ellsberg-poisoned atmosphere of the White House during the summer and fall of 1971 is reminiscent of the Kremlin during the late days of Stalin and the chimera of "the men in white." Nixon could not tolerate the *sight* of an opponent, even the most harmless and peaceful demonstrator with a sign. The specter of Philby (called "Philbrick" by the preparer of the transcript, who is obviously not very spy-conscious) seems to have haunted the President, as though he were a proto-Ellsberg in British pin stripes. Like Stalin, Nixon was meditating a purge, but because the U.S. was a democracy it would have to wait till after the election. In Washington, after the election, heads did not roll, as they did during the "doctors' plot," but Helms went, early in 1973, death had taken care of Hoover the previous spring, and late last summer a big "reorganization" of the CIA was reported. Ehrlichman, moreover (this has just now come to light), took a leaf from Yagoda's book: in 1971, he presented Admiral Welander with a prepared confession to sign that would have made "me admit to the wildest possible, totally false charges of political espionage." Welander refused.

Nixon's grim focus on Ellsberg is as easy (or as hard) to explain as Stalin's final paranoia, which combined his fear of assassination with a phobic suspicion of Jews to fix on the doctors around him, and then struck out at Soviet Jews in general. Anti-Semitism was latent in the Soviet

Union, just as red scares are endemic in the United States. Even Nixon, though, cannot have imagined Ellsberg as his future assassin except in a symbolic sense. The theft of those documents, their *exposure* to public view had dealt the presidency a wound, and Nixon, in his own mind, had merged with the institution, to become a single body. The publication of the Pentagon Papers planted in him a doubt of the inviolability of his person and the office and of the principle of "confidentiality" about which he evidently has deep-rooted feelings. It was as if his monitoring system, which he had hoped would give him total security in the Presidential ambit by putting whatever happened there *on record* for his own exclusive retention, had been defied, almost laughed at, by another set of records compiled under McNamara's directions and spirited away by a private individual.

At the same time there was perhaps something about Ellsberg, the man, the pre-Papers, clean, crew-cut Ellsberg, a defiant hawk in Vietnam, looking out, still, with a tight eager smile from the cloud of hair, that reminded Nixon of some of the younger "modern conservatives" in his own office family, and a sneaking suspicion of "knowing the type" would have further disturbed his balance, making him look fearfully at the aide with a clipboard coming in the door. Hence the angry insistence on Ellsberg as a "traitor" and the obsessive memory of Philby.

Late in the fall of 1971, the co-ordinates for Watergate were fixed, even if no brain as yet had made the calculation. The courts were preparing to try Ellsberg on two counts—theft and unauthorized possession of national defense documents—charges far too mild, in the White House view, for the gravity of the crime, and later beefed up to twelve, including espionage and conspiracy. After the unproductive Fielding burglary, the White House retained the Plumbers' "capability," in addition to Caulfield and Ulasewicz, but had no immediate interesting employment to offer them. Electronic surveillance, working out of Ehrlichman's office, had hardly been given a chance to show what it could do: only a few taps on journalists and on Kissinger's aides. Over at CREEP there was money to burn. In September, on Caulfield's recommendation, McCord was hired by CREEP as a security officer, part time. A former FBI and CIA operative, he had knowledge of "the art of certain technical devices . . . listening-devices and so on." Liddy, who arrived on December 10, did not; his field was clandestine photography. On January 1, McCord went on full time.

The idea of putting these elements together and plugging them into the campaign may have been Nixon's. If he dropped it into Haldeman's "suggestion box" during a chat at Camp David, it probably drew a neutral response: "I'll look into the parameters, Mr. President, and report back." Alternatively, Colson brought Nixon the idea, which he had thought up himself or which had come to him via Hunt from Liddy—he did not meet Liddy in person until early February. Or maybe several people, separately, put it forward. It is impossible to trace the routes by which it beat its way to Nixon's mind until finally it could not be dislodged. But some time, as early as December or as late as April 1, it achieved "worthwhile for go status." The conjunction of McCord and Liddy in the CREEP offices, followed by McCord's going on full-time salary—facts not subject to dispute—point to a Christmas birth date.

It is impossible to foretell whether Nixon will be removed from office, by one means or another, when Watergate celebrates its second anniversary. As I write, the prediction is that he will stay. Yet Watergate has a strange organic life of its own which, in my opinion, is more persistent than Nixon's desperate hold on power. Watergate has showed itself to be like an angleworm or a child's belief about an angleworm: if you chop it in pieces, each piece will wriggle off and make a brand-new angleworm. Last September, everyone was sure that it had died. Then came Agnew. After Agnew, another "dead" period followed. Then came the Saturday Night Massacre. Another brief suspension of breath, then the missing tapes, then the tape erasures.

This persistence is not an accident or just bad luck. Watergate returns, reasserts itself because it is a whole, consistent in all its parts like the angleworm. It is a creation of Nixon and of Nixonian politics. Agnew, strictly speaking, had nothing to do with Watergate, but because he himself was a creation of Nixonian politics, he was a parallel phenomenon that could not sustain scrutiny when brought out into the light of day.

This organic wholeness of Nixon and his works, faithfully reflected in Watergate, has produced some ironies, nasty tricks of fate. But the irony results from the utter consistency of the whole—there are no spare parts; everything returns on itself. Because of Watergate, for example, Dan Ellsberg has gone free. And if Nixon gnashed his teeth over that, he must at least have cursed when he read McCord's letter to Judge Sirica. What had persuaded McCord to talk or had been at any rate a prime factor in his decision was his loyalty to the CIA. On this point, he testified with a good deal of heat and at length. He was angry when he first heard of the White House effort "to lay the Watergate operation off on the CIA" and he had refused to go along with the suggestion that he use the CIA in his defense.

I could not use as my defense the story that the operation was a CIA operation because it was not true. . . . Even if it meant my freedom, I would not turn on the organization that had employed me for 19 years. . . . I was completely convinced that the White House was behind the idea and ploy which had been presented, and that the White House was turning ruthless, in my opinion, and would do whatever was politically expedient at any one particular point in time to accomplish its own ends.

I was also convinced that the White House had fired Helms in order to put its own man in control at CIA. . . . It appeared to me that the White House had for some time been trying to get control over the CIA estimates and assessments, in order to make them conform to "White House policy."

He went on to talk somewhat incoherently about how Hitler's intelligence chiefs had been obliged to lie to him in giving their estimates of foreign military capabilities— thereby losing him the war. Jim McCord was a fire-breathing patriot and seemed to have decided, post Watergate, that the White House, through persecution of the CIA, was weakening the country's defenses. It took all kinds of Americans, including the seven rather conservative senators, to bring out the Watergate story: the press, the judiciary (Judge Sirica), even Pat Gray of the FBI. Nearly all of Nixon's chickens have come home to roost, but a few more—the last of the brood—may finish the job.

March 7, 1974

Since these thoughts were written, the grand jury has indicted (March 1) seven of Nixon's associates and handed its sealed envelope to Judge Sirica. Watergate has come to life again, and again Nixon's days appear to be numbered. In Cincinnati, a Republican candidate has been defeated—another inroad on strongly held Republican territory. Senator Ervin's committee has been voted some more money. Nixon has said on television that when he told Dean "It is wrong, that's for sure"—his newest recollection of the words he used on March 21, 1973—he was talking about clemency for the men in prison. Not, as Haldeman had sworn before the Ervin panel, about raising a million dollars' worth of hush money. This would seem to "cover" Haldeman on one perjury charge: he had not been lying under oath to the Senate Committee but had only had a poor recollection of the context, understandable since hush money and clemency had been linked in the discussion. Nixon went on to say that some "individuals" (was he thinking of the twenty-three grand jurors?) who read the whole transcript or heard the whole tape might put a different interpretation on the conversation, but "I know what I meant."

We can now understand at least why the tape was not Deep-Sixed. The statement "It is wrong" or "That would be wrong" must occur somewhere on it, and to preserve those three or four precious little words, Nixon evidently decided to let the grand jury, if that was its mood, "misinterpret" the rest of the conversation: proof that he has a moral sense was scarce enough not to be jettisoned.

The seven indictments for conspiracy, perjury, lying to the FBI and the grand jury, obstruction of justice relate only to the cover-up. The grand jury apparently drew no conclusions as to who planned and directed the original crime, unless those conclusions are contained in the sealed envelope. One can hardly blame the jurors for failing to pronounce on the matter, since no hard evidence, so far as we know, pointing to the guilty party or parties has been produced. Those who had an interest in covering up are legion—virtually the entire Nixon apparatus—but the entire apparatus cannot be guilty of ordering the break-ins at the Watergate. The plain fact is that the cover-up is still going on: evidence, in the form of criminal knowledge, is being effectively hidden, justice is being obstructed.

The grand jury indictments only confirm what was already a certainty in most people's minds: that those seven men (though I must say I did not suspect Gordon Strachan) were lying and/or conspiring to conceal when they gave testimony to legally constituted bodies. But what is not yet a general persuasion, what we can only guess at, remains a secret shared among a handful of men, not more than four probably. Three of these are now under indictment, and the prospect of jail may serve to force some truth out. But it is more likely that the one who is still at large will be judged and condemned by another court—the Congress or what is left of the Republican party—before his accomplices stand up to hear the verdicts reached by their peers.

Postscript on the Pardon

September 9, 1974

This morning we heard on the radio that President Ford had pardoned ex-President Nixon for any offenses he might have committed while in office "against the United States." Immediately afterward came the announcement that Ford's press secretary and long-time friend J. F. terHorst had quit in protest. So Nixon is home safe at last. Though he may still be liable to prosecution for civil or state offenses, he will never have to answer for anything—were it high treason or forging Treasury bonds—he did during his incumbency in violation of federal statutes. Whatever his crimes, those imputed to him during the impeachment proceedings or others (who knows?) undiscovered and not yet even suspected, he is free for life from federal pursuit. And it looks as if his six associates or accomplices—the men under indictment whose trial was slated for September 30—are home safe too.

The argument most frequently heard against any kind of pardon for him, when that curious possibility began to be discussed, was the unfairness this would work on Haldeman, Ehrlichman, Mitchell, and company, of whom it could not be claimed, evidently, that they had "suffered enough" —as Ford declared of Nixon—in losing the highest office in the land. But now the principle of equality before the law, originally appealed to in the insistence that all the guilty should be punished, can be seen to turn around sud-

The Mask of State

denly and plead on their behalf. The injustice of their "paying the price," when the boss has not only been absolved but is drawing large sums from the taxpayers in the form of a pension and travel and office expenses, is bound to be visible to a nation of arguers schooled in points of equity. Should these men be actually tried and condemned, one can expect a furore reminiscent of the Calley case, with them in the piteous role of "scapegoats," "little fellows," who were only carrying out orders issued by their commander-in-chief.

On the other hand, if they are not tried, the net effect of Ford's action yesterday will have been a general absolution for all Watergate criminals still at large, which will be bound to seem unfair to those like Kalmbach, Segretti, McCord, Hunt, Liddy, and the Cubans, who have already been punished by doing time in jail. To restore impartiality, those still behind bars would have to be let out, by proclamation, and some handsome form of compensation—along the lines of Nixon's severance pay—devised to reimburse them for the time they have served. Magruder, who is reported to be studying theology in prison, will have to close his scriptures and partake in the general amnesty. And what about Nixon's nemesis, John Dean, who had just started serving his one-to-four-year term when Nixon got his absolution? Ford could reason, I suppose, that Dean alone deserves no compassion and should stay where he is till he too has "suffered enough," however that measure can be quantified.

Was this Ford's intention in giving his predecessor an "absolute pardon"—to set in motion a swift-acting process that would end by undoing all the work of Judge Sirica, Archibald Cox, Leon Jaworski, the grand jury, the Supreme Court, the Ervin Committee, the House Judiciary Committee, not to mention Frank Wills, the watchman at the Watergate who first gave the alarm, the three cops in the prowl car who answered his summons, the sleuths Woodward and Bernstein of the Washington *Post*, John Dean himself— everyone, large and small, who contributed to the nation- wide search for truth?

Possibly Ford has not yet seen where pardoning Nixon will lead. He is considered to be rather dull-witted and unreflectingly, bemused by sentiment, may have stumbled on a formula that the cunning Nixon and his associates might have envied for wrapping up the stinking Watergate mess and burying it with a single gesture, in full view of the public, with a stroke of the pen. Yet the emotional speech he made on television yesterday and which we can now study in this morning's papers seems to testify to a determined intention: "My conscience tells me clearly and certainly that I cannot prolong the bad dreams that continue to reopen a chapter that is closed. My conscience tells me that I, as President, have the constitutional power to firmly shut and seal this book." In fact, the Watergate "chapter" was not closed; much remains (or remained) to be known that, thanks to him, can now never be proven, established in a court of law. He proceeds in the same vein: "There is an American tragedy in which we all have played a part. It can go on and on or someone must write 'the end' to it. I have concluded that only I can do that. And if I can, I must."

One might ask: Why must he? What is his hurry? Whose interest is served in "sealing the book" at this point, before all the evidence has been heard, before Nixon has been brought to trial and subjected to cross-examination, before his co-conspirators have given their version in open court? For that matter, we cannot judge whether or not he ought to be pardoned unless we know what he has done or is supposed to have done, and it is just this information that Ford's untimely (or timely?) action has permanently sealed off from us.

Ford has been moved to act, he says, by the human interest of Nixon and his family, but also by the national interest, to forestall a trial that would cause "prolonged and divisive debate." Perhaps it would, but one wonders whether that was really what Ford wanted to spare the country. To judge by today's reactions and by terHorst's instantaneous resignation, Ford is already stirring up divisive debate by the pardon and above all by the timing of it: a presidential pardon *before* trial is almost without precedent, except in cases where a general amnesty was proclaimed, and lawyers even now are discussing whether such an unheard-of act is within the constitutional powers of the president, whether in fact it does not amount to interference with the judicial process—one of the very counts on which Nixon might have been indicted. It could even (though it doubtless will not) open the door to impeachment proceedings against Ford himself. Though he may hope, as Nixon did, up to the last apparently, that the storm he has provoked will blow over, at the very least he has suffered an appreciable loss in popularity—that all but universal popularity he bathed in during his first month in office and which was based partly on relief that the hideous struggle was over and partly on the surprised sense (it had been so long) that a normal cheerful mediocrity, instead of an abnormal cheerless one, was occupying the office. Now Nixon's pardon may cost Ford's party, which was riding high with him on the wave of elation, votes in the November Congressional elections, and even endanger his chances of re-election in far-off 1976.

So why did he do it? Let us start by believing him honest, or reasonably honest, and discard the notion of a deal: Nixon agreeing to go quietly if Ford would agree to give him an unconditional pardon within a stated lapse of time. If Ford was enough of a crook to participate in such a bargain, he would be enough of a crook to welsh on it, should he see fit, when the due date arrived, and deny it had ever existed. No, let us think he was sincere yesterday when he told of wrestling with his conscience, which implies that he was free to make the decision and not bound or influenced by any prior, under-the-table arrangement.

He cannot have been prompted by public opinion, for the polls were running 58 per cent against any kind of immunity for Nixon, 33 per cent in favor, and 9 per cent "Don't know." Another possible motive has to do with Jaworski, the special prosecutor. For weeks there has been a story in circulation that Jaworski had something big on Nixon, bigger than anything yet known, and was moving to indict him soon. If the story was true (and no doubt we shall some day know), Ford, informed by Jaworski of the facts, would have moved fast to protect the ex-president from unseemly exposure, that is, to steal a march on the special prosecutor. This would be understandable in human terms: Ford owed Nixon something—the vice-presidency—and hence might like to spare him, but how this crony behavior could serve the national interest is a mystery.

No evidence of wrong-doing held by Jaworski, no matter how fresh and juicy, could have greatly shocked or disarrayed a nation already stunned, early in the summer, by Nixon's own publication of the transcripts of some of the tapes of the presidential conversations: even his worst enemies had not expected him and his confederates, when among themselves, to talk like Murder Incorporated. After this, to learn of new gaps, apparently erasures, in the tapes turned over to Judge Sirica, to learn that the Nixon transcripts contained significant omissions and bowdlerizations, discovered by the House Judiciary Committee on listening to the originals, that campaign contribution funds had been diverted by Bebe Rebozo through several bank accounts to buy Pat Nixon a pair of diamond earrings, could cause no surprise and hardly any pain.

All through the summer, right up to his resignation and for weeks after it, if Nixon remained a puzzle or an unknown quantity to his compatriots, it was not for lack of evidence against him but, rather, because of the wealth of it: reading the transcripts in paperback, watching the proceedings of the House Judiciary Committee on television, people in America were asking two questions and, so far as I heard, two questions only: Why in the world did he make the tapes in the first place and why, when their existence became known, did he not destroy them? The simplest answer—blackmail, in both cases; he made them to blackmail his associates and retained them for the same reason —was not completely satisfying, perhaps because it was simple. Even Nixon loyalists (not counting the lunatic fringe) no longer disputed the evidence. Their line of defense now was that all politicians were the same, that if you had any transcripts of Johnson, you would hear how dirty he talked, that a Democratic senator's wife had accepted a fur coat, look at Chappaquiddick, look at Humphrey, and anyway, they liked his peace program, he got us out of Vietnam, didn't he, don't forget that, and wasn't he a friend to Israel? Meanwhile their numbers dwindled. The "silent majority" at last fell silent, just as, while we watched on television, his die-hard stalwarts on the House Judiciary Committe, finally aware that they had been betrayed by him, quietly faded away.

Had Jaworski been permitted to indict Nixon on the rumored graver charges or on still more detailed evidence than that before the House Committee, the likelihood is that this would have served to unify the country rather than divide it. Misgivings, perhaps natural in those who had believed in him so long, that the man had been cruelly hounded from office for offenses that in anyone else would have been considered venial, would have been laid to rest, and if a presidential pardon had come after trial and conviction, even his opponents might have felt that the time for mercy had arrived. The pleasures of picturing Nixon in jail have always been secondary to the desire that the true facts about him should be known and acquiesced in.

So whatever Jaworski has or had in his possession could hardly traumatize the country or, in Ford's phraseology, "polarize the people in their opinions" and "challenge the credibility of our free institutions of government . . . at home and abroad." That the spectacle of Nixon in the dock could be unpleasant to watch or read about is something else, but the simple plea of "guilty" would have obviated his appearance, except to enter the plea and hear the sentence. It is true that, given his character, one could hardly hope for this outcome: he has already withdrawn the mite of a confession that was wrung from him early in August when the Supreme Court decision forced him to hand over the clearly incriminating tapes of June 23 (six days after the break-in), which, as he admitted, were "at variance with certain of my previous statements." He also admitted concealing that fact from his lawyers and from the legislative body examining the case. Today he concedes only "mistakes and misjudgments." A man on trial who is incapable of perceiving what his own actions amount to is obviously a public embarrassment, but that man, Nixon, has been on trial, in reality, for more than two years before the court of public opinion and the television cameras, and our free institutions have not suffered for it, though there has been some amazement abroad. To prolong that trial, now that he has been separated from his official functions, and transfer it to a court of law—or to a judge's chambers— ought to have merits as well as painful aspects. At least the suspect would no longer be on view in his official *persona*, as head of state, under the scrutiny of other heads of state and their watchful entourages, alert for signs of strain as the grinning effigy shook hands, exchanged toasts, rose to deliver an after-dinner speech; citizen Nixon could concentrate instead on his defense, which is what he ought to do if he is confident of his innocence. At any rate, there is no reason to think that protracting the "ordeal" of Richard Nixon would be as disturbing to the nation as Ford is making out.

Something nevertheless must have gravely disturbed *him*, unless the words we heard this morning relayed by BBC were mere oratory. If we assume that he was speaking from the heart (and American politicians, on the whole, are highly emotional beings), we must conclude that he had had a scare. Something had impelled him to act, and as rapidly as possible, to remove Richard Nixon from the public eye. He must never come to trial. That must be averted at all costs, and a swift and total pardon, whatever the risk to himself and to the Republican party, seemed to be the only course: ". . . if I can, I must." If the price of Nixon's pardon would have to be amnesty for the others, he was willing to pay it. In fact, a blanket pardon would not only seem logical to the average guy; in the long run, it would be necessary to discourage civil lawsuits and keep Nixon out of the witness chair—there was a subpoena on him right now to appear in the September 30 trial and his pardon did not exempt him from the duty of being a witness. Executive clemency—an instrument that Nixon in the end did not dare use in his attempts at cover-up—was now Ford's prerogative, and, being without complicity in the Watergate matter, he could afford to dole it out on the principle of equal justice and fair shakes.

It is worthwhile examining Ford's language to try to divine what—if my supposition is right—had given him such a fright. ". . . I cannot prolong the bad dreams that continue to reopen a chapter that is closed." Whose bad dreams? He cannot mean America's; except for inflation, the country is in a state of euphoria. Nixon's, then. He is talking about Nixon, and the chapter that is closed is Nixon's presidency and the events that happened therein. Nixon, in San Clemente, keeps trying to reopen that chapter; he will not write "the end"; his mind returns over and over to the scene of the crime or, rather, to the "misjudgments" he made. He is in a squirrel-cage turning round and round.

Ford again: "There is an American tragedy in which we all have played a part." What tragedy? It cannot be Watergate, since most of us played no part in that drama, either as heroes or villains; we were spectators. And anyway, for us, it had a happy ending: Nixon went, and all his court with him. The American tragedy, or what Ford sees as a tragedy, is Richard Nixon. His rise and fall. He is a tragedy in himself, as a man, as well as in what happened to him, and in a sense we have all played a part in that: we voted for him, opposed him, cheered him, abused him, marched against him, strewed flowers in his path. We helped him on his way up, and when he started to fall, we pushed him. That is surely how Nixon looks at it in exile at San Clemente with his "bad dreams," which pursue him in a waking state and which may be mixed with intermittent brighter daydreams of a "comeback."

In the last weeks there have been newspaper stories of his

bizarre behavior at San Clemente: peculiar telephone calls to former colleagues on the Hill in Washington that seemed sometimes to imply that he thought he was still in office, vindictive tirades followed by apathy: we have had word-pictures of him poring over stacks of unopened mail, lonely walks on the beach, financial anxiety, fears of destitution; finally, and most oddly, as reported by the Washington *Post*, "inability to say the name of Leon Jaworski." "He is emotionally depressed," a visitor concluded. If all this is coupled with Ford's allusion yesterday to the former president's "health," one can suppose that Nixon is—temporarily or permanently—insane, in other words, that his mental condition, were he to be indicted, would not permit him to stand trial. No wonder that Ford, who has surely been receiving reports and may even have been telephoned by Nixon, feels pity and terror.

Here one can see, through Ford's eyes, where the interests of the country come in. If Nixon were committed to a mental institution (the normal procedure when a person under indictment is found unfit to stand trial), that could well affect the prestige of the United States, at least in the shocked view of its citizens. Royalty, since the office is hereditary, is allowed to go mad, but elected representatives, when they visibly crack up, are felt to cast discredit on the masses that voted for them. A history of mental illness, even an ancient history, as we saw in the case of Senator Eagleton, almost automatically disqualifies a vice-presidential candidate: the thought that a madman could succeed to the presidency is unnerving.

Luckily we have survived Nixon's tenure. But the knowledge, if it took the form of a legal finding, that he is presently of unsound mind would inevitably give rise to second thoughts about his previous condition. Were his actions while in office those of a sane man and did he merely go into a clinical depression on losing the office? There is no sure way, obviously, of establishing that. The idea that his mental disturbance is no new thing will be attractive a) in confirming old suspicions on the part of a minority and b) in clearing up for the general public some hitherto inexplicable features of his behavior. We would no longer seek rational explanations for the tapes mystery, why they were made and why he did not destroy them before it was too late; for his night visit to the student anti-war demonstrators at the Washington Monument to discuss football with them; for his strange remarks to Harold Wilson last spring and at Pompidou's funeral; finally, for the Watergate break-ins, if it was he who inspired and ordered them. The answer would be in our hands.

For liberals, sheer madness would help account for his more insensate and wicked acts, such as the Christmas bombing of North Vietnam, the Laos incursion, the scare alert, last fall, of the armed forces during the Arab-Israeli war, which was varyingly interpreted as a nuclear warning to Brezhnev and as a diversionary tactic in the tapes controversy. For the far Right, it would be clear, finally, that a grandiose lunatic in the White House had arranged the détente with the Soviets and the brotherly recognition of Red China. In short, all Nixon's policies and acts, from the SALT talks to "Vietnamization," would be subject to reassessment if it could be argued that a deranged brain had initiated them, and Ford might well have worried about the unpredictable consequences for the stability of our alliances and undertakings.

But this is not all. There is still Watergate. According to reports, Nixon is alternately silent and talkative. We can only guess at what he is saying, since he receives only trusted people of his own camp, but accusations are said to be frequent, and the theme uppermost in his mind seems to be Watergate. No doubt members of the House Judiciary Committee come in for quite a bit of abuse, but it is hard not to think that some of his old familiars—Mitchell, Colson, Haldeman, and Ehrlichman—are being railed at for what they did to bring him to this pass. In his verbal incontinency, lashing out right and left, he must be telling not all that he knows but more than is good for him. If he himself (as I continue to believe) was the guiding spirit and evil genius of Watergate, he is certainly, being Nixon, not proclaiming it, even *in extremis*, yet in casting blame wildly about, at the very least he must be revealing an intimate knowledge of what happened, spilling the beans with a vengeance (literally) and unaware, probably, of the extent to which he is doing so. In general, when any of us starts accusing others, he is likely to betray his own guilt, and Nixon can be no exception. Those who heard his disjointed farewell speech to the White House staff on television will not be surprised at anything this dissociated person may be letting fall at San Clemente.

The presidential transcripts published last June already show great unsteadiness of control: for long passages he seems to forget that the recording system is listening to what is said, then suddenly he will remember and revert to his public voice and to the authorized version of Watergate that presents him as utterly ignorant of what has been going on, a mere detached seeker of information. Then again he forgets. It is possible with a pencil to mark the points where this occurs. Not a word, however, is spoken— or at any rate appears in the transcripts—that indicates any foreknowledge of the June 17 break-in. There are several ways of interpreting this. Either he had no foreknowledge and was somewhat taken aback, as well as curious, or the tapes and portions of tape that disclose foreknowledge have been destroyed or partially erased, or in this particularly vital and dangerous area he was *always* mindful of the monitoring system.

It has been clear for a long time—more than a year—that we would not get the whole truth about Watergate, including the precise details of its planning, until one of the original nucleus of conspirators broke under the strain and began to talk, implicating his fellows, if not necessarily himself. But the last person from whom we would have expected this was Nixon. If in fact he has broken or was on the verge, Ford's swift pardon was a move to shut him up, straitjacket him, for his own sake, as well as that of the public, which in Ford's conventional view could not stand the shock of so much mud flying. "Lunatic" accusations by the former chief executive would inevitably have been followed by counter-accusations. Without sharing Ford's panic, I can feel a certain sympathy for him in his decision, the more so because I suspect the futility of it. That book cannot be sealed, as he ought by this time to know. If there is something in Watergate that keeps calling for cover-up, that can be summed up as the character of Richard Nixon. At the same time, there is something in Watergate—the same entity—that persists in disclosing itself, despite all efforts, well-meaning or evilly designed. Pardon will not quieten Nixon; nor in the long run will it defraud the public, if getting hold of the facts, the actual *corpus delicti,* rather than of Nixon's flailing, struggling person is its real desire.